Granddaughters of Corn

portraits of Guatemalan women

Marilyn Anderson and Jonathan Garlock

CURBSTONE PRESS

Special acknowledgements are due to the following publishers, individuals, and organizations for permission to reprint excerpted material (acknowledged in footnotes) from their publications: Anchor Books, Americas Watch Committee, Comité Pro Justicia y Paz de Guatemala, Cultural Survival, Inc., *Enfoprensa,* Epica Task Force, Four Arrows, Grove Press, Guatemala Human Rights Commission/USA, Guatemala News & Information Bureau, Iglesia Guatemalteca en el Exilio, Instituto Centroamericano de Documentacion e Investigacion Social, Ixquic, Marilyn Moors and Tracy Bachrach Ehlers, National Lawyers Guild, Network in Solidarity with the People of Guatemala (NISGUA), North American Congress on Latin America (NACLA), Organization in Solidarity with Guatemala (O.S.GUA.), Oxfam America, Parliamentary Human Rights Group, University of Oklahoma Press, and Women for Guatemala.

For permission to publish material resulting from interviews, thanks are due to Elena Ixcot and Efrain Marroquin.

printed in the United States
by Curbstone Press
paperback binding: Mueller Trade Bindery
MADE IN THE USA

Curbstone Press wishes to thank the many people whose support has helped to make this publication possible, with special thanks to Steven Welch, Richard M. A. Benson, and Mel Rosenthal for their support, help and encouragement.

This publication was supported in part by RESIST, and by The Connecticut Commission on the Arts, a State agency whose funds are recommended by the Governor and appropriated by the State Legislature.

LC: 87-71735
ISBN: 0-915306-64-6 (cloth)
ISBN: 0-915306-60-3 (paper)

distributed by
THE TALMAN CO.
150 Fifth Avenue
New York, NY 10011

CURBSTONE PRESS   321 Jackson Street   Willimantic, CT   06226

Acknowledgements:

In addition to acknowledging the many authors and publishers who permitted us to cite material in the text, we want to express special gratitude to a number of groups and individuals whose work, encouragement and assistance helped shape *Granddaughters of Corn:*

—   Women for Guatemala, the Guatemalan Human Rights Commission, and Americas Watch, whose efforts to document the repression led to lists of the disappeared;

—   The Secretaria de Ayuda para Refugiados Guatamaltecos, P.E.A.C.E.for Guatemala and CARGUA, groups whose work with the refugees in Mexico was critical to our understanding;

—   Elena and Felipe Ixcot and their family, Efrain, and all the Guatemalan refugees we've met and spoken with, whose courage and grief remain our inspiration;

—   The National Endowment for the Arts, whose 1976 Services to the Field award facilitated the photographic documentation of highland weavers;

—   Nancy Lorence, a friend and member of the New York City Committee in Solidarity with the People of Guatemala, who read and commented on early drafts and dummy layouts with the insight of one who has lived in and come to know and love Guatemala;

—   Judy Doyle and Sandy Taylor, who not only saw a need for *Granddaughters of Corn* but also shared the principle of working on a consensus basis concerning this book's editing, shaping and design;

—   Our friends and *compañeros/as* too numerous to mention, who read or viewed portions of the book in progress and whose responses spurred us in our effort to make a good accounting to the common people of Guatemala who some day will ask, in the words of their poet Otto René Castillo,

> "¿Qué hicisteis cuando los pobres
> sufrían, y se quemaba en ellos,
> gravemente, la ternura y la vida?"

> [What were you doing while the poor
> were suffering, their humanity and their lives
> consumed by flames?]

— M.A. & J.G.

Granddaughters of Corn

INTRODUCTION
by Jonathan Garlock

And they have caused him to disappear, in a way no other
man has done. I should not have sorrowed so long over his dying
if he had gone down among his companions in the land of the Trojans,
or in the arms of his friends, after he had wound up the fighting.
So all the Achaians would have heaped a grave mound over him,
and he would have won great fame for himself and his son hereafter.
But now ingloriously the storm winds have caught and carried him away,
out of sight, out of knowledge, and he left pain and lamentation to me.
                                        —Homer [Odyssey I]

Where do people who disappear go to?
Look in the water and in the high grass/
Why do they disappear? Because we're all not the same.
When do they return? Every time our
thoughts bring them back.

                                        —Ruben Blades[1]

In 1983 there began to appear in various publications about Guatemala lists
not only of people who had been murdered but of people who had been
disappeared. These lists grew, month by month, revealing circumstances of
the abduction of persons from every walk of life and of all ages, from Indian
campesinos in remote hamlets to *ladino* professionals in Guatemala City.
These people were detained by military or paramilitary personnel. Their
families did not know where they were or whether they were alive.

A surprising number of the disappeared were women. Whether these
violations of Guatemalan women's human rights were overtly political,
primarily sexual, or random and unpremeditated, they represent a pattern of
systematic abuse.[2]

When women were not being disappeared themselves, they were the
mothers, wives, sisters, daughters, lovers of disappeared men. Stories
emerged of the anguish and fortitude of these women as they made their
endless inquiries at hospitals, police and military headquarters, morgues
and cemeteries, government agencies. As with the Madres de la Plaza del
Mayo in Buenos Aires, whose struggle to disclose the fate of their

Of the approximately 4.5 million illiterate people in Guatemala, 55.7% are women.[3]

Amnesty International has concluded after a study of thousands of cases over a period of many years that the majority of political abductions have been carried out by currently serving and reservist members of all branches of the Guatemalan military and security forces, acting under the orders of their supervisors in the guise of so-called "death squads."[4]

As a consequence of the high rate of unemployment and under-employment — characteristics of a dependent capitalist system — thousands of Guatemalan women daily cover dozens of miles re-selling merchandise or working until late at night washing and ironing other people's clothes, in order to earn enough to feed their children. Many indian women survive in the city by making tortillas to sell. They send their children to deliver the heavy baskets of tortillas to the houses of their customers or, after doing this themselves they then go to the market to sell more.[5]

One woman, brought to Rabinal and held in the *destacamento* for almost a month, was raped over 300 times. . . When she left the *destacamento* for the army refugee camp, the same soldiers who had raped her gave her five pounds each of rice and beans "to start a new life."[6]

disappeared children — the MIAs of Argentina's "Dirty War" — led to solidarity and organization, the efforts of disappeared Guate-malans' families led to the formation of a mutual assistance group, the GAM.[7] Guatemala's then head of state, Mejía Victores, declared that "to take steps toward the re-appearance of the disappeared is a subversive act." In 1985 GAM Secretary Maria Rosario Godoy de Cuevas, who had joined the group because of her husband's disap-pearance, was killed along with her 4-year-old son and her 18-year-old brother.

Repression and violence against Guatemala's people is nothing new. The displacement, exploitation and massacre of Guatemala's indigenous peoples has a long and bitter history, dating from the time of Alvarado, the General of Cortez who conquered the Mayan peoples. During the three centuries — from the 1520s to the 1820s — that Guatemala was ruled by Spain the Indians' land was expropriated, the people themselves were subjected to strict controls, their labor was coerced through systems of tributary and compulsory labor. These exactions, imposed only with the ferocious cruelty recorded by Bartolome de las Casas (*Tears of the Indians*), together with the introduction of new crops and agricultural technology, were nothing less than an assault on traditional Mayan culture and its social structures.

The lot of most Guatemalans, especially Indian peoples, did not improve following independence from Spain. Throughout the 19th and early 20th centuries the country was ruled by a series of dictators, such as Cabrera and Ubico, while the nation's economy came increasingly under the control of British, German and United States interests. The key sector, agriculture, sustained by migrant Indian labor, came to be dominated by the production of cash crops for export: coffee, bananas, and later, cotton and cardamom. One company in particular, United Fruit, played a major role in the exploitation and control of Guatemala. As has been well documented and no longer is denied by the U.S. government, United Fruit, aided by the CIA, was directly responsible for toppling the democratically-elected government of Jacobo Arbenz in 1954 and installing Colonel Castillo Armas in power.[8] Ever since, Guatemala has been torn by political violence between popular resistance and military regimes and supported by the United States.

This violence intensified in the 1960s, with sporadic guerrilla resistance in both the cities and the countryside. Between 1965 and 1970 nearly 10,000 peasants were killed, chiefly in the eastern, non-Indian part of Guatemala. In the late 1970s the discovery of oil, nickel and other mineral resources led to a scramble for control of Guatemala's northern states. Land that had been held by various Indian groups since before the Conquest was expropriated. In protest a large number of Indians marched in 1980 to Guatemala City to petition the government. Their pleas were ignored and, to call attention to their plight, they occupied the Spanish Embassy. The Guatemalan army then attacked and burned the building, killing nearly everyone inside.

This event marked a turning point in Guatemala's political struggle. As opposition to the government grew — in part the result of deteriorating economic conditions — and as the participation of indigenous people grew, repression intensified. At first the violence was selective: union leaders, priests and catechists, students, teachers, and the heads of cooperatives were assassinated by death squads in increasing numbers. By 1980 Guatemalan newspapers regularly contained accounts of extra-judicial executions (such as the shooting of a primary teacher in front of his pupils), the discovery of mutilated corpses along roadsides and the seizure, detention and disappearance of civilians. Nearly 700 union officers and over 400 students and faculty of San Carlos University were murdered during Lucas García's presidency.

In 1982 the four principal groups leading armed resistance to the government formed an alliance, the URNG,[9] adopted a common program and

The significance of . . . popular movements for national politics became clear following the 1976 earthquake . . . After the earthquake, the government was incapable of directing the national reconstruction effort. Hence, cooperative members and slum-dweller associations sought independent aid from international relief agencies and began the process of local reconstruction on their own.

Just two weeks after the earthquake, the army began its "counter-insurgency program" in El Quiché. Members of the Catholic Action and the cooperative movement especially felt the blows of the government's terror campaign. Between February 1976 and the end of 1977, 68 cooperative leaders were killed in Ixcan, 40 in Chajul, 28 in Cotzal, and 32 in Nebaj.

The government's program of political violence became a means of suppressing the rural development that had emerged in Guatemala in the years before and after the earthquake.

The 1976 earthquake and the subsequent abuse of aid exacerbated a bad situation. . . The earthquake tore open many holes in the social fabric which had already been stretched thin. The rich and those in power came out richer and the poor came out poorer, and the differences and inequalities became more visible. More protest led to more repression to contain the forces of change. Those in power do not want to share the wealth.[10]

In our hamlet today almost nothing remains. It is dead, burned.[11]

"It was 9:00 at night. It was very dark and I couldn't see anything. I was resting in the hammock when all of a sudden I felt that an animal fell on top of me from the tapete. It seemed like a cat, but much bigger. I became frightened thinking it was a cadejo that had come for me. Its eyes were yellow and it looked at me. I couldn't sleep, and that's how I was all week. I consulted with the sahorin and he ordered me to put a glass of water under my bed, burn copal and put [out] many flowers. It was the spirit of my best friend that the army had killed and left on the road. I was afraid of the army and did not go to bury him, leaving the animals to eat him."[12]

initiated coordinated actions. Ríos Montt — who had seized power in a coup — then launched an indiscriminate military offensive against the civilian population. This campaign has been extensively documented by such agencies as Americas Watch, Amnesty International and the Guatemalan Human Rights Commission. The overwhelming evidence of testimony taken from witnesses and survivors points to a ruthless and systematic effort by the Montt regime to eradicate all opposition through a combination of random killings, wholesale massacres, intimidation and forced resettlement.

> The President of the United States is more President of my country
> Than the President of my country
>
> —Roque Dalton[13]

With the installation of Vinicio Cerezo the Reagan Administration has sought to portray Guatemala as a democratic nation which fully respects human rights. A decline in the number of disappearances and political murders following Cerezo's election in December, 1985, has been offered as justification for reauthorizing military assistance to Guatemala. Indeed — and as part of its effort to discredit and isolate the Nicaraguan revolution — the U.S. State Department has heralded Cerezo's election as part of a "wave of democracy" said to be sweeping Latin America. By this is meant the replacement of military with civilian heads of state and the restoration of political forms of representative democracy.

However, the human rights situation in Guatemala can be properly understood only in the context of a wave of repression that has swept Central America in recent decades. As two books recently published in English make clear — *Nunca Más* ("Never Again") and *Torture in Brazil* (originally published as *Brasil: Nunca Mais*) — the violation of human rights by regimes such as those of Argentina and Brazil during the 1960s and '70s was not aberrational.[14] It was not a question of military personnel and paramilitary operatives acting on their own or behaving with excessive zeal. Rather, their activities were coordinated through a systematic apparatus of repression created as an expression of deliberate policy: the Doctrine of National Security.[15] Formulated with U.S. assistance but rooted in national fascist movements of the 1930s and '40s, this ideology subordinates constitutional freedom and human rights to the absolute imperative of state security — defined by the military acting in the interests of ruling elites.[16]

These books demonstrate that widespread arrests, disappearances, rapes, tortures and murders are accomplished only with the complicity of the military, the judiciary, the government, members of the professional strata — among others — and that repression on this scale requires the commitment of significant resources (weapons, vehicles, places of detention) and trained personnel (security agents, torturers, doctors). They also reveal a collaborative network not only with U.S. military advisors but between Latin nations themselves.

There is little prospect that conditions will improve under Cerezo. Archbishop Penados' prediction that "the regime emerging from the [1985] elections will be a militarized civilian government since the military will not cease to wield power"[17] was an accurate assessment, especially in light of the military's increased direct control of the national economy.

Reports of a successful democratic opening in Guatemala must therefore be viewed with scepticism. While political violence may have shifted from army massacres of entire communities to death squad attacks on individuals, human rights issues must continue to be viewed in the light of a significant pattern revealed by Americas Watch:

> Reviewing the record we find that the Reagan Administration failed to condemn gross violations by Presidents Lucas, Ríos, and Mejía while each in turn held office. Indeed, at times, it praised their performance on human rights. As soon as a Guatemalan military dictator was deposed, however, the State Department condemned his human rights record for the purpose of favorably comparing his successor to what went before.[18]

Cerezo has already capitulated to the military by granting a blanket amnesty covering human rights abuses which occured prior to his tenure. Though he has obviously sought to prevent violent suppression of the GAM since it achieved international recognition, he has publicly and repeatedly repudiated their demand for accountability. In so doing he has avoided the central question posed by GAM: "Is it possible that democracy can be built on the basis of thousands of 'disappearances' and 'assassinations'?"

Over 25,000 children younger than six years old in 94 *campesino* villages in the Cantabal region, in the northwestern *departamento* of El Quiché, are in danger of dying of malnutrition and from lack of medical attention.[19]

I bury my hands in the earth
And seeds escape me
Like fleeting dewdrops in the field.
. . .
I bury my heart in the earth's center
And celebrate the fecundity of maizefields
Filled with bowing silken tassels
. . .
Let us love, then,
My silenced countrymen,
Deities whose ranks are swelled by hunger,
True keepers of the Mayan hearth.
Let us love, despite all odds —
Feel the full round of our clay's emotions —
For tomorrow, O Mayan people,
Grandchildren of corn, ancestors of my hands,
You shall inherit
The earth's scented perfection.

— Otto René Castillo[21]

GRANDDAUGHTERS OF CORN — first developed as the exhibit,
"Granddaughters of Corn: Women and Repression in Guatemala" — is a
response to the human toll taken by the actions of the Guatemalan military
over the past several years. Our decision to undertake this project was
confirmed by an extended interview with a Guatemalan Indian woman living
in sanctuary in the U.S. So much of her concern was for her *compañeras*,
the women who remained in Guatemala, threatened and intimidated, widowed
or orphaned, violated, and faced with the burden of sustaining their families
and preserving their culture.

In seeking to illuminate the hidden war in Guatemala — this third ring in
the Central American circus of violence in which Nicaragua and El Salvador
have been the main events — we decided to combine portraits of
Guatemalan women with information about the circumstances in which
hundreds of women had been disappeared and to contrast these images with
statistical data, testimonies, and reports. The portraits and other images in
the book come primarily from documentations we did of Guatemalan
weaving, both in Guatemala and among the refugees.

In 1975-76 we travelled to document traditional textile production
techniques, especially the backstrap weaving done in the highlands. Aware
that changes in traditional craft production were being accelerated by the
impact of industrial society on indigenous culture, we were anxious to
document as fully as possible the achievement of Guatemalan weavers.
Over a three month period we visited some sixty communities throughout the
highlands, compiling an extensive visual record of backstrap and floor-loom
weaving.[22]

16

The experience of those three months remains vivid. Arriving at a village we would enquire after weavers, often in the *mercado.* Since these were indigenous women, there was often the initial difficulty of finding someone who spoke Spanish; in many cases a young man who was bilingual would discuss our project with us and then introduce us to a relative — mother, sister, aunt. Frequently we would be taken to an *aldea* several kilometers from the village itself.

Marilyn would introduce herself to the weaver she wished to photograph. She would carefully explain the purpose of her project and from a box would bring out 8X10 black and white photographs from previous trips, showing women from other parts of Guatemala weaving on backstrap looms. Immediately she would be surrounded by women eagerly examining these photographs, commenting on the costume of the women portrayed and discussing these other weavers' techniques. She would then invite the participation of a weaver, assuring inclusion in the documentary record not only the craft of the individual weaver but the traditional technique of the community. With few exceptions, women allowed themselves to be photographed at their looms.

At least 75,000 *quintales* (3,750 tons) of beans which the government has stockpiled in National Institute for Agricultural Commercialization (INDECA) warehouses have rotted, stated Agricultural Minister Humberto Mancur Donis on April 16 [1985].[23]

Appropriately, Marilyn's photographs played a significant role in persuading weavers to participate in the project. Through these images, weavers could see that she understood weaving technique, that her concern for their craft was genuine, and that her work was craft.

Sometimes a weaver's technique could be documented in an hour or two but where the technique was complex or conditions difficult — Marilyn used only natural light — a session might last an entire morning or afternoon. During this time there might be interruptions from children, other family members, curious neighbors. Often the weaver would stop to explain a step she was performing. As she worked, we would ask about the source and cost of her materials, get estimates of the labor involved in production, learn whether pieces were made for personal use or for sale, inquire how the weaver had learned her craft and how long she had practiced it . . .

By the time she was ready to pack her cameras, Marilyn had established rapport with the weaver. And then, almost invariably, the weaver would shyly ask if she might have her portrait taken: a photograph not of her at work at her loom but showing her as she wished to be seen *as a person.* She would disappear into her tiny adobe or thatched home and reappear

45% of Guatemala's population is under 14; life expectancy at birth is 49 years.[24]

The Ixtacapa and Nahualate rivers, in the southwestern *departamento* of Suchitepéquez were poisoned recently, killing fish and crustaceans, *campesinos* from the area told reporters on April 15 [1985].

The *campesinos* explained that the rivers run through an area where the army is engaged in counter-insurgency activities and that the poisoning affects many *campesinos*.[25]

after a few moments, her hair combed or bound with a *cinta*, wearing her best *huipil* and *corte.* She would then present herself to the camera, standing erect before her home — perhaps with one of her children — and look into the lens with an almost shattering directness.

Thus the weaving documentary project resulted in two distinct sets of images: a comprehensive record of the weaving techniques of highland Guatemala and an extensive series of portraits. The technical images formed the core of a study, *Guatemalan Textiles Today,*[26] and constituted the nucleus of several photographic exhibits at museums and galleries. Although a few portraits were included in the book and those shows, to provide context, we only gradually came to recognize the portraits as a vital document in themselves. The outgrowth of an effort to document weavers' work, as well as of relationships that developed between weavers and photographer, the portraits constitute a special record. First, because of their intimacy: in a culture hostile to the curiosity and often exploitive intrusion of outsiders, Marilyn was welcomed and encouraged to create extraordinarily personal images. Second, because of their historical significance: many of the communities in which these portraits were made have since been disrupted or destroyed during years of civil strife.

In April, 1983, we visited Mexico to investigate the situation of Guatemalan refugees in Chiapas. Reports from Guatemala in 1981-82 had described escalating violence throughout the countryside. In October, 1982 — four months after the event — the *New York Times* recounted the army's massacre of the entire population of *finca* San Francisco — over 300 people. About the same time stories began to reveal a major exodus of refugees into Mexico and we saw the first news photograph from a refugee camp, showing Guatemalan women wearing the costume of communities we knew well.

In the headquarters of refugee assistance groups in San Cristóbal de las Casas we observed maps showing over thirty camps located along the Mexican-Guatemalan border. Unable to reach the camps in the remote and mountainous selva we interviewed people engaged in providing aid to refugees In these camps, saw photographs they had made, read testimonies they had received. We also saw drawings made by the children in these camps, which graphically depicted the violence they had experienced.[27] Many of their villages had been attacked by helicopter. Often the men of a hamlet had been rounded up and murdered by the Guatemalan army. Entire villages had been burned to the ground. Large numbers of people had abandoned their homes and survived for weeks in the jungles and mountains of the border region. Many refugees, in a state of severe hunger and shock, had died soon after their escape to Mexico. The survivors lacked food, shelter, clothing and medicine.

We were able to confirm this picture by visiting Santa Rosa — a relatively accessible camp near the Guatemalan border. Because of its location the basic needs of these refugees could be met fairly well. Still, conditions were extremely difficult. Several hundred people, chiefly women and children, were crowded onto a few acres of *ejido* land which the Mexican peasants — themselves Mayan Indians — were allowing them to use. The refugees lived in cane huts with thatched or corrugated plastic roofs but no walls. They had little fuel with which to cook and few utensils. Unable to grow food, they were virtually dependent on relief aid. They had no regular work, either in the fields or in the camp, to perform. They had few personal possessions and, despite large numbers of children, few playthings. There was no teacher, no priest. Almost without exception the women had

It is very difficult to liberate oneself. To see one's ideas change doesn't happen overnight. And it is hard to change your mind-set, for that is how you were raised. I believe that it is a collective struggle. You do what must be done so that you can continue to change. For instance, our women's work group has done a lot for me because, among my compañeras, I am able to see my problems and my failings. If one is alone it is extremely difficult, especially with men running the show.[28]

In the early 1970s, 48.8% of the rural work force were semi-proletarians, while 41.3% were rural proletarians in the strict sense, owning no land of their own. . . 83.3% of the economically active population in the countryside earn 34.8% of the total rural income; 1.8% of that population receives 40.7%.[29]

abandoned their *traje,* either selling it to obtain money or forsaking the most visible part of their identity to avoid problems with the Mexican authorities.

Because many in the camp were from a Guatemalan community we knew and they were able to recognize friends and relatives in photographs we brought with us, these refugees had confidence in us and were quite

frank in revealing their personal experiences. We were struck by their incomprehension of the motive of their tragedy. Over and over we were told in sad, bewildered tones that Ríos Montt was "mad," "insane," *"sin competencia".* In their trauma these refugees resembled villagers we had met in 1976 following the earthquake — victims of an ineluctable natural disaster. While some in the camp had a clear analysis of their situation, many still failed to grasp that the inhabitants of an entire village could be murdered as an act of state terrorism.

In still another situation where refugees were able to earn income through craft and other projects, we observed a loom with an unfinished cloth into which were woven the poignant words, *"Donde Iremos"* — "Where will we go?" The Mexican government, to its credit, has resisted Guatemalan demands that the refugees be repatriated. Many have been moved from the border region to camps in Yucatan and Campeche, but most remain in Chiapas. Others, unwilling to be relocated in areas far from Guatemala, have fled into the jungle along the border. Many have left the camps and live as undocumented persons in Mexican communities, especially Mexico City.

Twenty percent of the dwellings in the areas of conflict are un-inhabited, and the whereabouts of their residents unknown.[31]

"So long as we haven't swept everything that's Indian from the face of the earth, so long will there be neither peace nor rest in this beautiful land."

> — *General From the Jungle*
> B. Traven [32]

When we were in Guatemala in 1980, we met an artist who had cut up and photographed a beautiful handwoven *huipil*. The image of the mutilated cloth was intended as a metaphor of what was happening to that country, especially its Mayan people — to show that the fabric of their society was literally being torn apart.

Since 1965 40,000 Guatemalans have been disappeared. In a country of only 8 million people, during the past twenty years 100,000 have died in political violence. Over 1,000,000 have been displaced by the army and now live in Model Villages (i.e., strategic hamlets), in communities other than their own, or in hiding; more than 150,000 are refugees in Mexico. There are 36,000 widows and over 125,000 orphans. Some 800,000 Guatemalan men have been pressed into Civil Patrols, used for paramilitary service and forced labor.[33]

It is clear that President Cerezo will not enact significant land reform or restore lands confiscated from indigenous peoples, enforce the minimum wage law, dismantle the model village program, or even mount an effective campaign against illiteracy, hunger and inadequate health care. Yet the U.S. Press has been favorable to Cerezo, lauding him for alleged human rights improvements and, most recently, for hosting the meeting that produced the Arias "Peace Plan" for Central America. He has also been portrayed as something of a victim, a man of great decency who would right wrongs — such as the failure to prosecute those responsible for thousands of disappearances — if his hands were not tied by the Guatemalan military. Cerezo, however, is the architect of his captivity: in a pamphlet published in 1977, *The Army: An Alternative,* Vinicio Cerezo himself suggested that:

> Progressive politicians and military officials have a joint responsibility in the destiny of these countries and that both sectors must share the nation's decisionmaking. . . Only two sectors could direct such a process [developing the country]: a progressive political party, with a wide popular base, discipline and an awareness of its historic task — like the Christian Democrat Party; and an organization which has the right technical formation in the values of discipline, order and the exercise of power — like the Guatemalan Army. . . There will be no positive solution unless the two sectors UNITE and make a gigantic and combined effort to reorganize and reorient the country.[34]

Thus, while Cerezo may be an improvement over the caudillo Ubico (1931-1944) who proclaimed "I am like Hitler. I execute first and give trial afterward", or General Ríos Montt (1982-1984), who asserted "We are not

In looking at the human rights situation in Guatemala people are always comparing numbers. And obviously, if we compare statistics . . . But that isn't the problem! It isn't a matter of comparing numbers, because the [Guatemalan] government is simply unable to continue to commit massacres for years on end. It is impossible! They cannot sustain a politics of massacres. The numbers now are therefore not the same. You cannot compare 1982-1983 with Vinicio Cerezo and what is happening now. They have changed tactics, initiating this process of the "democratic opening" — which is really an institutionalization of the repression.[35]

killing Indians, we are burning Communists",[37] the struggle of the Guatemalan people for freedom and dignity is likely to continue for many years.

The resistance of the Guatemalan people takes many forms, ranging from almost daily skirmishes between guerrillas and the army to the protracted struggles of industrial and agricultural unions, neighborhood associations, church groups. It includes the highly visible protests of the GAM and the reformist program of Father Giron to purchase and redistribute under-utilized landholdings. It includes the day-to-day efforts of thousands of Indian people, though forced to live in Model Villages and to serve in Civil Patrols, to maintain their values and their culture.

It embraces, too, the Communities in Resistance — small, linked highland groups which have chosen neither to flee to Mexico nor to join Model Villages but instead have developed forms of agriculture, organization and defense appropriate to a highly mobile existence. Some observers consider these communities' terrain to be embryonic liberated zones.

The resistance includes the determination of exiled peasants in Mexican refugee camps to rebuild their shattered lives, to survive, to remember and, some day, to return.

And it includes the efforts of exiled priests, labor leaders and peasant organizers, artists and others, who have built a network of human rights and support groups which publish to the world the largely-hidden story of today's Guatemala and which provide material aid to the victims and the opponents of that country's tyranny.

During a trip to Mexico in September, 1987, we spoke to many refugees — in the Chiapas camps, in San Cristobal de la Casas, and in Mexico City — and met with several human rights, humanitarian and solidarity groups. We were able to observe the spirit of these people, to learn in detail of these groups' work. And it is our impression that a new Guatemala is indeed being born.

In the camps people from different Indian groups are learning to work together, to overcome the barriers of language and custom which, together with distance, had separated them. They are beginning to inter-marry. Their children sometimes speak Spanish as well as one another's language. Weavings are losing some of their traditional colors and designs and are borrowing new combinations.

Images of the transformation:

— A scene from a videotape made about the Communities in Resistance showing several women from different highland groups, each wearing her distinctive *traje,* weaving and conversing together.

— Human rights workers interpreting Guatemalan history to a group of people in their twenties, mostly European, during an orientation for International Peace Brigade members on their way to Guatemala, where they would accompany GAM members in an effort to safeguard their lives.

— Two Indian women — one from Chajul, the other from Chichicastenango — weaving in a Mexico City apartment; dressed in jeans and blouses, one wearing heels; sitting on tubular metal chairs, backstraps around their waists and the ends of the warps tied to the window-post; chatting in Spanish.

— The women of one refugee camp, ladinas who had never woven in Guatemala, weaving on backstrap looms the art they had learned from Indian refugee women.

— A group of refugees gathered around a recently-arrived marimba, where men just back from cultivating corn and collecting wood were practicing a traditional tune — in a camp appropriately named "El Porvenir" ["The Future"].

We dedicate *Granddaughters of Corn* to this future, to this new Guatemala, and to the aspirations and struggle of its people.

Rochester, New York
November, 1987

It is important to state that these photographs are not specifically of disappeared women. Rather, the women in these portraits represent their disappeared sisters, underscoring the reality that every name listed on these pages is that of an individual as real as the woman looking into the reader's eyes.

The woods growing on the slopes of the Atitlan volcano, in the *departamento* of Sololá, "have been subject to a moderate forest fire for the last two days," reported the radio news program *Patrullaje Informativo* on March 29 (1985). According to the local inhabitants, the army, which is carrying out military operations in the area, set the fire. The woods had served as a communal resource for the villagers.[38]

The ceiba (*Eriodendrum vesculifolium* H.B.K.) is still a sacred tree and is preserved whenever possible when the forests are cleared. To the Indian it symbolizes life. The ceiba represented the center of the twelve cardinal points, which together made thirteen, the sacred number among the Maya. This tree was believed to have its roots in the earth, its trunk above the horizon, and the top in the sky. It was called the "tree of council." Under its branches the village councils were held, for the wise men of the tribe claimed to derive inspiration from its roots. Indian dignitaries were elected under it. It was also believed that from the roots descended the Indian race. Even now, on special occasions, the roots are decorated with rose petals and *pom* is burned near them. The ceiba symbol may be seen on the *huipiles* of San Pedro Sacatepéquez.[39]

"440 villages . . . the army now acknowledges were destroyed in counterinsurgency operations in 1982-1983."[40] Listed below are the names of over 360 villages where massacres, bombings and other army violence have been recorded:[41]

Alta Verapaz:
Panzos
Yalpemech
San Cristóbal Verapaz
Sacatalp
Las Pacayas
Crumax
San Isidro
Rancho Quixal
Chiyuc
Pacoj
Paca
Tioxa
Chitun
Chitnij
Najtilagnaj
San Marcos
Rubalchoc
El Rancho
Pambach
Santa Cruz Verapaz
Sacataljil
Cisiran
El Rancho Quizal
Chirequiche
Los Carrizos
Chirripe
Salacuin
El Sauce
Panpache
Pocola
Tactic
Chisec
Coban
San Pedro Carchá
Cuxpemuch
Penas Blancas
Semuy
San Jose Siaja
San Pedro Himlajacoc

Baja Verapaz:
Chitucán
Nimacabaj
Río Negro
Chichutak
Paxjut
Plan de Sánchez
Xocox
Buena Vista
Patrixcán
Agua Fria
Raxput
Concul
Xeabaj
Chichupaj
Cumatzas
Chategua
La Cumbre

Chimaltenango:
Patzal
San Martín Jilotepeque

Pachay las Lomas
Sacalá las Lomas
Panchala
Panimac
Chuatalún
Xesuj
El Molino
Estancia de la Virgen
Chicocón
Chipil
Pacoc
Pataj
Pachan
Tziquinay
Varituc
Los Chayen
Chuabajito
Sargento Chisoc
Santa Anita las Canoas
Patzaj
Saqua
Chuquel
Xeatzán Bajo
Patzun
Chimaltenango
Patulul
Pujumay
Las Colmenas
Xeatzán Alto
Agua Caliente
San José Poaquil
Santa Apolonia
Chitún
Chipiacul
Parramos
San Juan Comalapa

Chiquimulla:
Jocotán

El Petén:
Melchor de Mencos
Belize
Macanche
La Union
El Cruzadero
El Zapote
Bonanza
Flor de la Esperanza
El Arbolito
Josefinos
La Libertad
Macanche
Palestina

El Progreso:
San Antonio la Paz

El Quiché:
La Estancia
Chiché
Cheputul
Santa Rosa Chujuyub
Macalajua
Uspantán

El Copón
Chutuj
Chimel
Chajul
Pol
Tzicojach
Finca Covadonga
El Mangal
Chel
Juá
Amachel
Chilele
San Gaspar
Chacalté
Namaj
Parramos
Bitzich
La Trinitaria
Santo Tomas Ixcán
Santa María Tzejá
Kaibil-Balam
Santa María Dolores
Los Poligonos
San José
Playa Grande
Xalbal
El Subin-Vista Hermosa
Las Dos RR's
Santiago Ixcán
Santa Cruz del Quiché
Centro Bethel
Cocob
Xesic
Sumal Chiquito
Xoraxaj
San Bartolomé Jocotenango
Cuarto Pueblo
Chinique
Xacebal
Chocorrales
Semejá I
Semejá II
Xesic Choacaman
Chitatul
Tabil
Cahijal
Macalbaj
Pueblo Nuevo
Cuevas
Xoljuyub
Ximbaxuc
La Vega de las Flores
Chupol
Chucalibal
Chuhueca
Chujalimil
Xajkulu
Lacama I
Lacama II
Agua Escondida
Chugueza II

Saquilla II
Patzibal
Chuchicapa I
Chichicastenango
Xepol
Chuabaj
Chijtinamit
Canjojal
Xepocol
Nebaj
Panasmic
Itzaabal
Tzalbal
Pajiya
Santa Maria
Suctziguan
Kosonip de Tzalbal
Ixtupil
Sajtziguan
Chorroxac
Chonana
Las Violetas
La Pista
Salquil
Patzul
Chichel
San Juan Cotzal
Cajixay
Namona
Cancap
Biochemal
Tupal
Guacamayan
Bichivala
Chenla
Vivitz
Technoc
Potrero Viejo
San Antonio Sinaché
Zacualpa
Pajaratuy
Pichiquil
Txununul
Guantajua
Parraxtut
San Andrés Sajcabajá
San Pedro Jocopilas

Escuintla:
Almolonga
Pinula
Champas Pinula
La Libertad
Las Cruces
Tiquisate
La Gomera

Guatemala:
San Juan Sacatepéquez

Huehuetenango:
Ocante
Pacantal
San Tomas Mayalan
Acal
Chamaxa
San Juan Ixcoy
Finca Piedras Blancas

Ixcán
San Mateo Ixtatán
Huaxic
Petenac
Xocultac
Chemican
Tsalaja
Selep
Jotbojoch
Julej
Llano Grande
Río Seco
El Poblado
Finca el Triunfo
San Miguel Acatán
Santa Teresa Olvido
Libertad
Coya
Lajcholaj
Covadonga
El Quetzal
Camnajchí
Cana
Nacapoxlac
Quilii
Petanchim
Mujuval
Icalquijal
Xémal
Lo Barranca
Tojlate
Tixel
El Olvido
San Francisco Nenton
Yaltoyas
Yalcatan
Aguacate
Yalambonoch
El Carmen
Canquintic
Chanquejelve
Guaxcana
Ixacacao
La Laguna
Chaquial
El Limon Chaquial
Las Palmas
San Jose Chaquial
Subajasun
La Trinidad
Txojbal
Yalisjau
Yuxquen
Jom Tzala
Quixal
Xoxtal
Palua
Nenton
Chajon
Chemal Mutixial
San Ildefonso
Arenal
El Limonar
Nueva Catarina
Nojoya

El Coyegual
Santa Ana Huista
Ojo de Agua
La Montana
Buena Vista
El Cajon Cuilco
Islam
La Democracia
Las Chulas
Chamaxú
Papal
Acal
San Antonio Huista
Chiantla
Capellanía
San Jose las Flores
Mixlaj
Palo Grande
Pichichil
Xenaxicul
Caserio Cruz Chex
Las Majadas
Llano Coyote
Coya
Nubila
Chimbán
Santa Teresa

Quezaltenango:
Estancia de la Cruz
Las Cuevas
San Juan Ostuncalco
Concepción Chiquirichapa

San Marcos:
Sacuchum Dolores
San Francisco el Tablón
San Pedro Sacatepéquez
San Cristóbal
Carusal
Tajumulco
Chalquitis
Taquian Grande
Totara
Pueblo Nuevo
Montecristo
San Jose Belice
San Miguel Tepajapa

Santa Rosa:
Chiquimulilla

Sololá:
Santiago Atitlán
Chuacús
El Adelanto
Pajujil
Concepción
Nahualá

Suchitepéquez:
Suchitepéquez
Mazatenango
Finca San Pedro
Río Bravo

Totonicapán:
Patubila
Xipuac
Santa Lucia la Reforma

The term "disappearance" itself first entered the international human rights vocabulary from Guatemala, where it emerged as a dramatic and massive problem in the 1960's. The initial wave of "disappearances" occurred there as a part of a counter-insurgency campaign against the first major guerrilla movement to emerge in the country. Since then, under successive administrations, the sophisticated counter-insurgency apparatus originally developed to deal with specific target groups has been utilized over a period of more than twenty years to quell any form of political and social opposition.[42]

There have been 38,000 *desaparecidos* in Guatemala in recent years, a figure equivalent to 42.2% of the 90,000 *desaparecidos* throughout Latin America, according to figures published by the Seventh General Assembly of the Central American Human Rights Commission (CODEHUCA).

The Guatemalan Human Rights Commission alleged a "qualitative increase" in human rights violations during the first half of 1985 and that the situation "deteriorated more all the time."[43]

The following are recorded names of women who have disappeared in Guatemala between January, 1983 and August, 1986:[44]

27

Herlinda Fajardo, 80 • Patrocinia Choc Bac, peasant • Juana Coc, peasant • Lucía Cam Poc, peasant • Patrocinia T
28 peasant • Ely Véliz M. • María Mitchell, 17, student • Máxima Barillas, 66 • María Dolores Rodas, 44 • Alicia Mejía
María Herlinda Godínez, 80 • Irma Burgos Campos, 46 • Lily Turton • Lucía Chuc, peasant • María Chuc, peasant • Al.

cía Romero • 3/83: María Aylón, peasant • Ingrid Lieserke, 19, student • Mariana Xujur, 24, peasant • Francisca
zalez, 18 • Cristina Choj, peasant • Mirna Lemus F., 19 • Inés V. Ramírez, 17 • Eugenia Ortega R. • Ingrid Valenzuela 29
4/83: María Juárez Aguilar • Miriam L. Ordoñez, 23 • Elvira Rosales, 41 • Lorena Morales, 18, student • María

Some disappeared four or five years ago, and some GAM leaders now express doubt that their husbands are still alive. "We had so much hope in the beginning," one of them said. "We even made jokes about what we would do when we got our husbands back. But for the past eight months, I've begun to believe my husband is dead."

Another member was blunt: "I know my husband is dead. How could he be alive after all this time? Now, my energy is for the GAM."

Others maintain hope. In an open letter published by Isabel de Castanon to her husband, Gustavo, she wrote:

"Keep going! Fight to survive in that secret corner, and here we will continue fighting for your freedom, because they will never, ever be able to make honorable men vanish into thin air, as if they were nothing."[45]

Ríos Montt inaugurated a "disappearance office" in the national police headquarters where "families could report the details of those who had been abducted." The office functioned for several months drawing hundreds of hopeful families to its doors. Not a single case was resolved, however, and some speculated that the office had been set up with the specific purpose of gathering more information on the relatives and acquaintances of those abducted. When Ríos Montt was ousted by General Oscar Humberto Mejía Victores in another military coup on August 8, 1983, the office was abolished.[46]

Cecilia Altopa, 40 • Flor de María Calderón, 18, student • Rosemary Aguilar G., 11 • Edmé A. Quiroa, 28 • Eva E. Polo, María Concepción Reyes, 27 • 5/83: Rosa Estela Villaseñor, 25, student • Ingrid M. Gómez • Bernarda S. Paz • Castillo C. • Alba García C. • Elvira V. Gutierrez, 56 • Ana Griselda Gutiérres, 26 • Blanca E. Castro, 21 • Hermin.

ero, beautician • Concepción Hernández, 35, vendor • Patricia Morales, 20 • Gloria A. Morales, 22 • Claudia Morales,
or • Laura Escobar, 39 • Dora A. Pineda, 1 • Blanca Luz Molina, 27 • 6/83: Yolanda Ochoa, peasant • Lucrecia Orellana,
ersity professor • Betzaida Lang G., 22 • Angela Ayala, social worker • Eva Ramírez, 21 • María Olimpia

31

33

"The first child in my family to be killed died there because of the poison sprayed on the coffee plants. After my brother died, my mother, who was picking coffee, kept him on her back the whole day. She waited until she had weighed the coffee before she put him down and we buried him in a hole we dug behind the shelter where we slept with the rest of the workers from our village. None of them reported my brother's death because the boss would have fired all of us on the next day."[48]

"On the fincas . . . the woman has to get up at 3:00 a.m., grind the corn for tortillas for the entire family for breakfast and lunch (which is eaten in the coffee field). A little later she must go with her husband to the finca to work alongside him. If the work is in the coffee field the woman must carry the 80 lb. coffee bag on her back at the same time she is carrying the baby in her arms and leading one or two other little ones. She must work from 6:00 a.m. until 2:00 p.m. After eating she must carry the 80 to 100 lb. coffee bag for 3 or 4 hours to the house of the finca owner. Then she returns to her house, makes a fire with wood and makes the supper of tortillas and maybe beans for her family. The woman doesn't know what it is to rest. All of her life is to work."[47]

The Guatemalan government is selling large quantities of powdered milk, donated by the U.S. non-governmental relief organization CARE for the nourishing of poor children, to pasteurizing plants, ice cream makers and retailers in general. On May 12 (1985), dairy farmers made this allegation before judicial authorities in San Jose Pinula in the Departamento of Guatemala, reported the television news program *Aquí El Mundo* on May 13.

According to the report, government warehouses are being used in the illegal sale of the milk.[49]

teacher • 10/83: Emilia Aguilar Hernández • Sandra Nineth and her daughter • Lucila Ubalda, peasant • Flor de N
34   Pinzón, student • Carolina Muñoz, student • Dominga García • María Elena Cifuentes, student • Julieta Sánchez, tea
• Maritza Fino, beautician • Carlota Arias • Celia Chet, student • María Cotal • Aura López, student • María

• Floridama Estrada • Ana Lucrecia Osorio, student • 1984: Julia Concepción Borrayo de Meneses, disappeared Jan
2, after leaving her house in Guatemala City • Ana Elida Girón, age 8, disappeared in Guatemala City, Januar
Emetria Marroquín • Irma Elizabeth Rivera, crockery seller, and Azucena Gómez, vendor, disappeared in Guate

"Where we lived, in the aldea of La Estancia, corn was the most cultivated crop. Corn is the most important thing we Indian people have. For us, corn is virtually sacred. Corn sustains our life because it is our basic food. During the rainy season I cultivated corn with my father. We sowed the corn. When the young plants started to grow we did the first weeding. Then we heaped up earth around the plant stalks. Eventually, with the passing of time, we harvested." [50]

Between March 16 and 26 [1985], 800 regular and special army troops *(kaibiles)* destroyed more than 400 hectares of maize crops in the Tzalbal village, *municipio* of Nebaj, *Departamento* of El Quiché, and in the surrounding area, reported the Committee of Campesino Unity (CUC) on April 9.[51]

Reason vanishes in attempts to explain why . . . a social worker is kidnapped by the army and found dead two days later, her body horribly mutilated and raped. If wanting to help people eat better by teaching them the five major food groups is a crime or a revolutionary activity, it is only indicative of the utter madness one witnesses in Guatemala.[52]

January 7 • Lorena Ramírez, minor • Ana Maria Ordoñez, 27, disappeared in Guatemala City, January 9 • Rubia
ia, teacher • Albertina Díaz Girón, 28, disappeared in Guatemala City, January 11 • Marcelina Hernández, and her
ren, Thelma and Lilian, disappeared from Guadelupe Cotosé, Escuintla, January 14 • Marta Mena de Dariani • Brenca   37

Paz • Sonia Elvia Livar Carranza disappeared in Zone 1, Guatemala City, January 31 • Roxanna Rodríguez, disappeared on the way to the National League Against Tuberculosis, Zone 1, Guatemala City, January 31 • Car Elizabeth Salazar de Cobos, 34, disappeared from zone 19, Guatemala City, February 3 • Ana Paiz de Peralta, 65, te

"I had gone to visit one of my sisters. On my return, only a half block from home, I saw a vehicle under the shade of a tree. It was a green pickup with the license plates upside down. As it was a little late, I felt afraid, thinking it might be a situation involving drunken men. As I was passing alongside the vehicle, the back door opened and a man got out. I swerved to let him pass. At that moment I turned my head and saw that he had a gun pointed at my shoulder. I was surprised and said to him, 'Hombre, Hijo de Dios, who do you mistake me for? I am a peaceful person. I have harmed no one. Let's talk.' I came back to identify myself to him but at that instant he shot me with the first bullet.

"I was hit in the right arm. I began to cry for help. I was in front of the house of a lieutenant in the military reserves named Victor Gomez. I shouted, "Lieutenant, Lieutenant, they are shooting me!" But the fellow who shot me and the others inside the vehicle had no intention of fleeing. I was shot a second time and wounded in the muscles of my left leg.

"Thus wounded, I continued to cry for help. Still on my feet, I managed to walk. I sat in the doorway of Lieutenant Gomez's house and then I saw who was shooting at me and I recognized him. It was the son of Señor Castillo Vasquez. His name was Rudy Israel Castillo Rodriguez, a member of army G-2. Seated by the door, this young man turned to pick up a gun. He leaped, military style, and landed in front of me. Balancing one arm on his knee he aimed his gun at my chest. He shot me the third time and fled with the other men in the vehicle." [53]

nia Areli Santos, 17, and her sister Maribel, 5, disappeared from Zone 19, Guatemala City, February 7 • Juana García, Juana Juárez, 55, nurse • Sandra Carranza, 25 • Andrea Alvarez, 84 • Irma Yolanda López de Ortíz, her husband uel Ortíz Barahona and their 5 children were abducted by National Police in Mixco, Guatemala, February 8; the

39

children were later released • Norma Padilla, Director of Fine Arts • Zaida Yvonne Avila Velíz, 14, and Zoila Nineth (
name unknown), 15, disappeared from Zone 7, Guatemala City, February 10 • María Yol Quell • Inéz Irasema R
Escobar, 22, beautician, disappeared en route to Kaminal-Juyu, Guatemala, February 14 • María Berrera • Ana Ca

• Inés Fuentes • Judith Franco Hildago, 14, student, disappeared February 16 • Noemí Galdemez • Leticia Ramos •
a Lidia Samayoa Ramírez, 21, law student, abducted by armed men, Zone 11, Guatemala City, February 19 • Marina 41
z de González • Minors: Aracely Quiñonez, Aracely López, Norma Pérez, Zoila Torres, Vilma Quintanilla, Argentina

Women cannot leave their villages to go to another village in order to earn a little extra unless they have permission to do so. If they express a desire to leave, they are suspected of working to supply the guerrillas. It is impossible to earn enough in one's village because everyone is so poor and to have more than necessary is seen as storing for the guerrillas. [54]

"Everything that the campesino uses in the field – fertilizer, mattock, machete – is expensive. We need to be able to bargain, but in the stores they have fixed prices. Everything the campesino produces has a very low price. How are you going to make a living?

"This is what I told the market administration when I was brought in by two policemen: 'You do us an injustice. We aren't here for the fun of it. We're selling our own products. We aren't selling drugs or marijuana. It isn't contraband.' And the administrator stood there gaping. 'Please don't go on talking! Go, but don't ask such high prices anymore.'

"But when I returned to my place in the market again, I began to talk with my compañeras. 'It hurts me a lot to see all that they are doing to us. They tax us when we come to the market, we have to pay bus fare and there are still other expenses. Almost nothing remains afterwards. You'd think we worked for pleasure, rather than from necessity!' I told this to my compañeras. Later people told me that what I said was very dangerous. 'It could mean your death.' " [55]

Vargas • Zoila Amparo Monroy, 30, disappeared, Zone 7, Guatemala City, February 20 • María Higinia Galindo • Ad
42 Villasinda and Marta López Barrios, abducted when 100 heavily armed men forcibly took the villages of La Colo
Morales and La Liberación, El Tumbador, San Marcos, February 21 • Lidia de Vélez • Irma Yolanda Tejada Mora

...ppeared after leaving her home in Guatemala City, February 21 • María del Rosario Morales • Evelyn Elvira Vásquez
...ra, 11, disappeared en route to typing class, Zone 18, Guatemala City, February 22 • Nancy Elizabeth Reyes Taylor
...her father, Jorge Rodolfo Reyes Hernández, disappeared on the road to Escuipulas, Chiquimula, February 29 •

Norma Aquino • Luz Haydeé Méndez de Santiago, 36, disappeared by armed men in a white truck, Guatemala City, Ma

44 9 • Carmen Salazar, peasant • María Ramírez, 36 • Blanca Castro • Reyna Suyapa • Rasaura Veliz Lima, 35, taken a⌐
by armed men in Oratorio, Santa Rosa, March 11 • Mayra Castro • Judith Castro • Isabel López, 18 • Guadelupe

In another case, reported to Americas Watch in early 1985, a woman was told by an army officer that her husband was still alive, and that if she slept with the officer, he would arrange for her husband's release. She complied and her husband turned up dead shortly afterward. [56]

"For a wife there will be concern for her husband or the grandchildren . . . Women will always have to be thinking of what will happen to their relatives or to themselves; it's something they cannot escape. In the concrete cases, where the repression has affected women, either killing the husband or the children, in those cases the women will have to carry on the economic work by themselves, as is happening in the rural communities in which there have been so many massacres. There are so many widows and they have to take on themselves all the work of providing food and maintaining the family . . . Also, the discrimination against women makes it even harder for all of them. I would say the situation is very hard, as never before." [57]

"Guatemalan women now play the part of both father and mother. Their husbands have been killed or their sons kidnapped." [58]

The majority of Indian and poor ladina women who move to the cities find work as domestics, "girls" as they are disrespectfully called. In this situation they are exposed to all kinds of abuse. They have no work schedule but carry out a variety of tasks from early morning until night and receive a miserable salary of $25 a month. The families that employ them insult and abuse them and even make use of them sexually. For these women there are no laws that permit them to organize or even that protect them. Indian women who work as domestics are obliged, because of their environment, to become "ladinoized", thereby losing their ethnic identity and becoming absorbed by the dominant ideology. [59]

As it is often necessary for families to obtain some extra income in order to survive women are obligated to begin working during childhood. 12.6% of the child labor force (between 10 and 14 years of age) is made up of young girls. The rest are involved in domestic work, condemned to the slavery of working more than 15 hours a day. [60]

The average life expectancy of Guatemalan women is very low, especially in rural areas where one can find young women 20 years old who look as though they were much older. Malnutrition, misery and hard work quickly cut short their youth. [61]

Michellana, 20 • María Pérez • Martha Zaiba, 19 • María Teresa Orantes, 20 • Thelma Cifuentes • Ana María Girón, 2
46 Alma Osorio, 25 • Brenda Elizabeth Ochoa García, 18, disappeared after leaving her home, Zone 5, Guatemala City, A
4 • Dora Izabel Quezada, taken by armed men, Zone 7, Guatemala City, April 4 • Ana Esperanza Chajón Flores, 18, F

"I didn't know anything — nothing, nothing of what was going on. Then in 1978 one of the nuns took me to Guatemala City. I began to read newspapers. From that time, little by little, I began to wake up. I began to understand how much the rich of Guatemala were exploiting the land. We Indian people understood nothing, nothing of the situation. We saw that we were victimized, enslaved. They treated us worse than animals. In clinics, in hospitals, they didn't treat us like Ladinos. Once I went to a hospital in Quezaltenango. There were other Indians there. It was typhoid fever; in some nearby *municipio* everybody got ill with it. A number of them couldn't speak Spanish. Some spoke Quiché, others Mam. I wanted to help them because I speak Spanish. I couldn't understand Quiché. But I saw them being insulted. It made me very sad to see how we were treated as though we were not brothers. We are all brothers.62

ool student, disappeared from her home in Zone 21, Guatemala City, April 15 • Gloria Estela Umaña, 24, her children,
and Dilicia, and Elia Vanesa Bolaños Umaña, disappeared from Puerto San José, Escuintla, April 18 • Lucrecia García, 47
dragged from her home by unidentified men, Zone 6, Guatemala City, April 18 • Maria Rosalia Kiloj, her husband, and

A 23-year-old woman, from San José Poaquil, Chimaltenango, the mother of two small children, described the army's reaction to her denunciation of her husband's kidnapping by the army on August 2, 1984:

"I went to the *destacamento* three times – the commander came over and said, 'Are you sure that I was the one who went and took your husband?' 'Yes, sir, I am sure because you were the one who came to the house,' I told him. Then he said, 'Okay, you go to jail.' They put me in the jail at eight in the morning; I was in there with my two babies until nine at night. There in the *destacamento* the lieutenant took out his pistol – he wanted to kill me. I told him, 'Look, sir, thank you very much for wanting to kill me; you took my husband and I don't want to keep suffering. But first kill my two children and then kill me so at least I'll have some peace of mind; I wouldn't want to know that my two children were wandering the streets alone.' And with that, they didn't kill me."

This woman had been raped repeatedly in her home the night her husband was kidnapped.[63]

In the first week of February . . . units of the army carried out searches in the villages of Papachala, Patzaj, Panimacac.

When the troops were in Papachala, soldiers snatched a newborn baby from its mother's arms and began to play soccer – with the infant as the ball.

The villagers could not contain their indignation and, unarmed, attacked the soldiers.

By the time the shooting stopped, 168 Indian men, women and children were dead. The bodies were hauled away – 15 truckloads of them – and dumped, later to be discovered because of the smell of the decomposing flesh.[64]

Carmen de Morales, domestics, detained and disappeared by heavily armed men during the night from their hom
48 *Zone 7, Guatemala City • Ramona Morales Guzman, 54, disappeared after leaving her home in Zone 7, Guatemala Ci*
Elizabeth Orellana, cashier at "Los Pollos", and three other women employees, dragged from their work by Nati

e, May 6 • *Gloria América Martínez, 19, barmaid, dragged away by unidentified men who broke into the bar where*
worked, Santa Lucía Cotzumalguapa, Escuintla, May 13 • Margarita Rodríguez de Valle, teacher, dragged from 49
ch by men on May 18, Suchitepéquez • Ana Edelmira Ixcaraguá Ixchajchalá, 28, abducted on the road to El

Salvador, Guatemala City, May 28 • Mélinda Ramírez de Bravo, teacher, disappeared from her house, village of Be
Santo Domingo, Suchitepéquez, May 20 • Nely Rodríguez Avila disappeared by unidentified men on May 20, villag
Rosario, Puerto Champerico, Retalhuleu • Irma Marilú Ichos Ramos, 23, disappeared by armed men in Guatemala

ARGO COMMUNITY HIGH SCHOOL
LIBRARY

21 • Maria Villanova Rompich Chiquín, 22, teacher, disappeared between Zone 19 and La Patría School, Guatemala
. May 21 • Edna Concepción Ramos Esteba, 18, disappeared in Zone 7, Mixco, May 26 • Georgina Chávez, 19, 51
opeared when she went to visit a friend in Zone 15, Guatemala City, June 3 • Tania Elizabeth Herrera Rodríguez, 16,

More than 800 women were raped by soldiers from the military base of Zaragoza, Chimaltenango, during August and September [1984]. According to a secret report of the army, 500 of them, the majority minors, are left pregnant. About 80 women were treated at "Centro Medico", a private hospital in Guatemala City, for injuries from rape.[65]

"In the destacamento . . . they rape women – the soldiers . . . They didn't do anything to me. But there was a girl they brought in there who they were raping every night. Fifteen soldiers more or less would rape her. The poor girl screamed; she was unmarried. They raped her; they even kicked her mother three times in her mouth. They dragged the mother and the daughter . . . the mother didn't want to let them (rape her) but they said, 'Get off lady! Because here we're going to split her apart.' . . . That's how they took her off. Another soldier was sleeping there and another over here and they put another soldier in between in front of them . . . They don't feel any shame anymore. So one woke up another and said, 'Get up, stick it in.' When he finished, he would put on his pants again and go, and then the other (would do) it to the girl. One would go and the other would wake up and he'd tell him to keep doing it to the girl. The poor thing was shouting – all night long. I was crying and praying because if my daughter should come down – the one who fled –I hope she isn't brought down to the destacamento because there they'll kill her. They'll kill her by raping her. They're not people anymore."[66]

bilingual secretary student, disappeared in Guatemala City, June 17 • Thelma Judith Flores Lemus, 17, student, abduc
52 by unidentified men, Zone 5, Guatemala City, June 12 • Indira Sayonara Aguilar García, disappeared in Guatemala C
June 24 • Edna Conchita Ramos Alvarado, disappeared in Guatemala City, June 26; she was pregnant at the tim

abeth López y López, 10, disappeared in the hamlet of San José, San Andrés Villaseca, Retalhuleu, July 1 • Bárbara elda Arauz Cetina, abducted by unidentified men, Zone 19, Guatemala City, July 2 • Yolanda Consuelo Rodríguez aga de Cardoza, 54, and Dina Patricia Cardoza Rodríguez, wife and daughter of Gen. Secretary of the Nucleus

The Panzos Massacre occurred on May 29, 1978. The Kekchi people had always lived in this valley of the Polochic River in Alta Verapaz, even before oil, nickel, copper, uranium, and antimony had been discovered nearby.

Little by little the Kekchis had been pushed from their lands. But the week before the horror, there had been a new series of bloody deeds, threats and an increase in military personnel. Those who lived in the village of Cahaboncito received a military order to go to Panzos, where they would receive a document answering their complaints about land seizures. They chose a Monday, May 29, to go. With them were Kekchis from nearby San Vicente. Upon arriving – perhaps 800 in all – they were directed to the plaza where, they were told, Mayor Walter Oberdich would reveal the news from the capital. The town was full of soldiers.

Witnesses say that then the soldiers blocked the exits from the plaza. A delegation of landowners was there to meet them . . . They began insulting the campesinos, threatening them with death. (One) said he had authorization "from the President and Minister of Government to kill you all."

The meeting had hardly begun when some Kekchis asked to speak. This was not permitted. Suddenly, perhaps in response to a scuffle between two soldiers and a man who did not speak Spanish, soldiers and civilians alike began firing on the unarmed Indian crowd from the rooftops. Men, women, children fell in their tracks.

The firing lasted only a few minutes as survivors fled screaming. Some died there in the park, others in the narrow streets where they fell. Still others were found bleeding in the cornfields.

At least five terror-stricken women holding babies had jumped into the hot and turbulent waters of the Polochic and had drowned.

After the first volley of gunfire, the rest of the attack was directed by (one) plantation owner, who rode around in a jeep with a lieutenant of the army. Later, he interrogated the wounded to obtain names, using a tape-recorder for later reference.

In the plaza, the bodies were left for hours where they fell. Medical assistance was denied the wounded. The area was sealed off to the press and to medical assistance. At 3 p.m., the bodies were loaded together into two garbage trucks and dumped into a common grave that had been dug by a bulldozer two days before the massacre.

At least 68 bodies – including nine women and ten children – were thrown into one pit. Forty six seriously wounded people, including ten women and eight children, died soon after and were buried in a second pit.

When news of the massacre reached Guatemala City, tens of thousands of people took to the streets, chanting in front of the Presidential Palace, "Cowards! Assassins!"

The Government made its official reply: 38 subversives, agitated by Fidel Castro, leftist guerrillas, and the clergy, had attacked an army garrison at Panzos, and had been killed. (Panzos did not have a military garrison)

More than 140 persons are known to have died.

At least 300 persons were injured. The Army brought in helicopters and reinforcements to comb the mountainsides looking for the wounded to finish them off. How many died of their wounds, frightened and in hiding, and how many were killed by their hunters – besides those who died in the plaza – probably no one will ever know.[67]

Direction of the Guatemalan Workers Party, detained and disappeared by the army while traveling by bus betwe
54 *Quezaltenango and Guatemala City, July 2 • Mirna de Aceituno, taken away while shopping, Zone 1, Guatemala City, •*
12 • Lidia Roxana Chinchilla Bol, 14, disappeared from Villacanales, July 15 • Francisca Rivera, abducted by unidenti

on the road to Taxisco, Santa Rosa, July 15 • Mirna Sayonara Vivales Girón, 15, intercepted on a walk and taken

y in a car in Mixco, August 13 • María Carlotina Arena, taken away by unidentified armed men while walking with 55

husband, Mixco, August 14 • Francisca Regina González, 47, clothes salesperson, abducted and taken away in a car

while waiting for a bus in Malacatán, San Marcos, August 15 • Hortensia Pazos de Martinez, 27 • Vilma Elizab
56 Esteban Matías, 9, disappeared from Zone 16, Guatemala City, August 20 • Carmelina Monzón Cruz, 10, and Evangel
Monzón Cruz, 6, taken away by unidentified men in a car, Las Francas, Jutiapa, August 20 • Rosa María Leiva Cuel

taken away in a car from in front of her house, Zone 3, Guatemala City, August 28 • Maria Magdalena Rivas de
té, 32, detained-disappeared by men who took her out of her home and drove off in an unknown direction, Zone 1
emala City, September 1 • Hortencia Pazos de Martínez, 27, disappeared on her way to shop in Zone 5, Guatemala

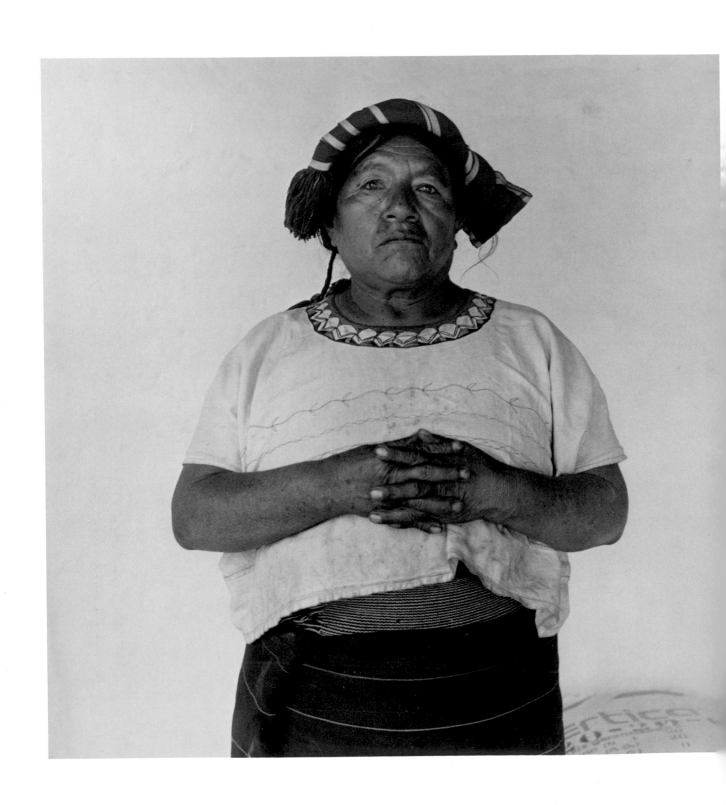

City, September 10 • Antonia Espinoza, 24, and daughter Cecilia Agustina, 9, detained-disappeared in aldea of Las Ve
58 Zacualpa, Quiché, September 10 • Dora Faustina Leon Vegas, 15 • Olvina Chan Montero disappeared in San Benit
Petén, September 14 • Lily Gonzalez de Marroquin, disappeared when she left the house on errands, Guatemala

"We do not want a graveyard peace (*paz de cementerios*) or a peace of disappearances," said Archbishop Prospero Penados del Barrio on June 3 [1984], during a religious ceremony held at the metropolitan cathedral to pray for the disappeared.[68]

n Chichupac . . . an entire family as murdered – "two men, a woman, nd two children. Two little girls. hey left them dead there; the animals ate them."[69]

n December 1983, Mr. Napoleon lfaro, General Secretary of the evolutionary Party . . . said that in e areas of conflict there are now 76,000 people widowed, 136,000 them women, which indicates an quivalent number of deaths. . . Vhat] was worrying Mr. Alfaro as how these dead persons were be regarded on the electoral lls.[70]

Vomen who have been widowed n't even have time to observe e traditional period of mourning r their dead husbands. Immed- ely, they must assume the tire burden of supporting the nily and feeding their children, 10, in addition to being orphaned, o suffer hunger and malnu- ion."[71]

People need to bury their dead, Lore Aresti, a psychologist, explains . . . "because that is a way of knowing where the body of one's loved one is, to know that it is there and not somewhere else, that the corpse didn't disappear, that it wasn't robbed, that there is no more suffering. When I can say, 'that is where he is, his name is Ruben and he's buried here,' then in some way I am vetoing death. 'Here is Ruben, he was the father of my children and I love him.' I am giving him his place, his name . . . and a tombstone, with his name inscribed on it. History will not take that away from me. Someone once said that society becomes civilized when it names its dead and establishes funeral rites. 'This is a citizen. He existed and he is here.' "[72]

ember 15 • *Rosa María Anleu de Salazar, her husband (Univ. Dept. Head) and their three children, disappeared in Datsun between Panajachel and Quezaltenango, September 27 • María Pérez Sirin, 15, disappeared after leaving house, Zone 7, Guatemala City, September 23 • Dora Faustina Leon Vega, 15, disappeared in September, when she* 59

"They came dressed as soldiers . .
They tried to lift my son by the legs
– they broke his knee. My poor son
They looked for machetes – two old
ones – and they went and cut his
throat. I came down crying. And
on the way down, they tore off my
necklace – one that had a pretty
cross on it. White silver . . . One
soldier who was behind me grabbed
me by the throat and broke my
necklace . . . This necklace that I'r
wearing belonged to my daughter;
put it on. My daughter, my child, m
little girl."[73]

"They killed a teacher who lived
very near to us. Her father was
blind. She was killed, machine-
gunned. Other friends were killed
different ways. Some were killed I
chopping off their heads. In La
Estancia there are two small lakes
and in them there appeared heads
floating on the water, the bodies
thrown upon the shore."[74]

"The army left. But before leaving
the military commandant, head of
the Huehuetenango/Quiché area,
shouted at the people: 'The next
time the guerrillas kill another sol
dier here (San Juan Cotzal), we w
kill all the men – you people bring
problems. And the next time, sixt
women. And the next time, sixty
children.' "[75]

left her house for the market in El Centro, Santa Rosa • Olga Patricia Hernández, 13, and sister Alma Graciela Hernár
60 4, disappeared while they were washing cars, Zone 1, Guatemala City • Elizabeth Vasquez Hernández, 19, disappe
    when she went out for her daily gymnastics, Guatemala City, October 8 • Victoria Miranda, daughter Feliciana F

...nda, and Rosa Ramirez Miranda were detained-disappeared in Malacatán, San Marcos, October 10 • Victoria ...les • Amanda Aviles, secretary, disappeared when detained by men who stopped her as she left work in Zone 1, 61 ...emala City, October 18 • Mercedes Lopez Garcia, 23 • Dolores Mey de León and her son, Pantaleon, disappeared in

The brutality which preceded each massacre simply demonstrated the total contempt in which the military hold life and that they instill the same contempt into the soldiers who carry out the crimes under their orders. A massacre leaves a trail of devastation behind it: not only are the population killed — men, women, old people, young children, pregnant women, usually after they have been subjected to the most vile forms of torture (burnt alive, machine-gunned, mutilated with *machetes*, children dashed against rocks or trees, victims buried alive, etc.); the houses are plundered and vandalised; money and essentials like household utensils are stolen; women and young girls are raped in front of their families before being killed; crops are burned or sprayed with toxins; the population are machine-gunned from helicopters and planes; bombs are dropped; water and food supplies are poisoned and there is evidence in some places of the use of bacteriological and chemical pollutants. This policy of mass extermination is directed against all communities thought to be providing political and social support for the *guerrillas* or simply suspected of doing so. This has also led to mass migrations by the survivors of these massacres, and other communities have managed to escape before being attacked by the army and paramilitary groups.[76]

What does it mean, "signs of torture?" Cadavers are found without eyes, testicles, or with hands cut off. Bodies are found without fingernails, teeth, or nipples. Women's bodies appear with chests burned, brands from hot iron on their skin, and with their scalp pulled off. Amputated parts are placed on top of bodies. Now you know what "signs of torture" implies.

Signs of torture: needles through the tongue. In the testicles. Stuck in the bottoms of the feet. Chests crushed by people jumping on them. Spikes driven and screwed into heads. Suspending the victim with nylon cord tied to his sexual organ. Amputation of the tongue.

Signs of torture: ears cut off. Drowned in gasoline. Face mutilated. Hands cut off the children of victims. Bodies have been found with genitals swollen "like footballs."[77]

On December 5, 1982, following a meeting with President Reagan, Ríos Montt told reporters: "We have no scorched-earth policy. We have a policy of scorched Communists."[78]

Mazatenango, Suchitepéquez, October 31 • Lila Noemi Gutierrez, 14, disappeared in Guatemala City, November 3 • I
62 *Yolanda Delgado, 26, and son Eddie Israel Samayoa, 6, disappeared on the road between Amatitlán, Guatemala,*
Chiquimulilla, Santa Rosa, November 5 • Olga Elvira Gomez Juarez, 17, taken by 4 armed men in Quezaltena

ember 8 • Ana Maritza Castellanos Monterroso, 15, disappeared in Guatemala City, November 11 • Margarita Garcia
a teenager named Juana disappeared while looking for work, Guatemala City, November 12 • Linda Oralia Morales, 63
ined with her husband, Irenio Mayen, by men who forced both into a car but later abandoned Mr. Mayen, Nov. 15 •

Sonia Marina Cortez Valle, 17, high school student, disappeared in Zone 8, Guatemala City, November 21 • Julia Loe 18, driven away by unidentified men, Zone 12, Guatemala City, November 23 • Leticia Guzman, 17, her sister Elizabeth, 13, and their brother were detained-disappeared by unidentified men in a car, Mixco, November 27 • E

At birth 41.8% of children weigh less than 5.51 pounds. This figure partly explains the high mortality rate among children: of every 1,000 children born, 161.5 die at birth. Only 35 of every 100 children live as old as 15 years.[79]

Three children scavenging for food on an enormous rubbish mound in the capital city were buried and killed by an avalanche of rubbish, rescue teams reported on February 11 [1985]. According to reports, children in the capital seek food in public dumps in order to survive.[80]

n de Nájera, Carlos Nájera, Isaura Hernandez de Nájera and Inez Nájera de Ramírez were abducted at night by
ily armed men, in aldea Santa Inéz, San José Pinula; Inez, age 60, was later found dead, having been tortured •
ria Moralles was disappeared by armed men in La Reforma, San Marcos, December 5 • Herminia Rodriguez, 49,

65

66 disappeared as she went to go shopping, Zone 3, Guatemala City, December 28 • Mercedes López García, 23, abdu
by heavily armed men, in aldea El Peñoncito, El Progreso, Jutiapa, December 28 • 1985: Emma Julieta Sánchez Med
13, her cousin Dolores Medrano Cambara, and a child of 18 months, taken away by heavily armed men, Guatemala

The killing of children in the Guatemalan highlands has taken on, on the army's part, a special racist aspect. "We have to get rid of the source of these communist Indians," has been a common phrase used by the army during its operations. [83]

A local inhabitant of the village of Río Bravo, Suchitepéquez, was walking home late at night when he tripped over the head of a partially buried corpse. When they started digging around the head, bodies of 10 victims, most of them indigenous people, were unearthed. They had been slashed with machetes and strangled, while four showed signs of having been buried alive. A few days earlier, 25 peasants from Solola had disappeared. [81]

"They left the poor mothers hanging, one with a little baby on her back. Three other children were on top of her, hanging. They strangled them; they cut the throats of the little ones. Some of them, they grabbed by their arms and stoned them against the floor, on their little heads. My husband buried them. You can't leave them for the dogs to eat." [84]

Editorial in *Impacto*, October 15, 1983: "Hundreds of times we have been taken aback by (newspaper) photos of cadavers surrounded by children smiling at the camera, as if the death itself did not mean anything. Years ago, our youth was still affected by the sight of someone who had been murdered, but now it seems that nobody cares, as if (death) were the most natural thing in the world." [82]

"Why did the army come to kill people there? Well, the army – the soldiers – came because they said we were guerrillas, that we gave them food and that perhaps our husbands were guerrillas, and that the whole village were guerrillas. Thus, they began to kill in the village. In many cases, entire families were murdered." [85]

ary 1 • Amabella Lizbeth Rivas Contreras disappeared on her way to high school, Zone 7, Guatemala City • Irene orga Quevado, housewife, left her home on February 5 and never returned, Zone 12, Guatemala City, • Cecilia t Ixcoy, disappeared after she left her house in Amatitlán, February 11 • Aura Marina Vásquez and other youths

67

Newspapers published the official figures for the number of orphans in three rural provinces – a staggering 51,000 orphans. If the other provinces are included, the final figure is estimated to be 100,000-150,000. As one Guatemalan journalist put it simply, "Guatemala is now a country of orphans."[86]

Back in Guatemala City, the general situation was compared to the bad old days of General Lucas García in 1982. Students, teachers, trade unionists and leaders of the displaced were being picked off the streets or taken from their homes at a higher rate than in 1983 – disappearances are running at 80 a month and political killings at over 100. It is the depressingly familiar story of people reappearing seldom, or only as corpses dumped in the street or down some ravine. Elections for the Constituent Assembly last July have changed little. "The government talks of the democratic opening," explained Nineth de Garcia, wife of Fernando Garcia, the minutes secretary of the glassworkers union kidnapped last February, "but how can they talk of democracy when so many of our relatives are still simply vanishing?"[87]

attending a movie disappeared in Guatemala City, February 18 • Rosa Amelia Samayoa Santa Cruz, Cristina Cabrera
68 Recinos, Vanessa Cabrera, Federico Godoy Santa Cruz, and five unidentified people riding in a truck driven by Fede
were intercepted by armed men who took them off in other vehicles, Zone 12, Guatemala City, February 20 • Car

iguez, 38, and her husband, Asst. Mayor Francisco Romeo Yoc, were taken from their house by unidentified men, in rio Trinidad Tajumulco, San Marcos, in February • Victoria Zapeta Matzar was detained and disappeared by 69 ntified men as she walked with a friend in Colonia Miraflores, Zone 11, Guatemala City, March 3 • Ana Vásquez, 9,

"When I was nine I had to go do the wash at 5:00 in the morning and at 7:00 I returned and left the laundry for my grandmother to hang and by 8:00 I was in school. Some days I had to go to have the corn ground in a nearby village, a kilometer away; we didn't have a mill in our hamlet. We didn't have electric light in our hamlet. It took me from 5:30 to 6:30 a.m. to get the corn ground and when I returned my grandmother had my breakfast ready for me and I went off to school without having studied my lessons at all. In spite of this I never fell behind. But I only stayed in school three years. Later the nuns gave me a chance to study more but I couldn't because I was needed in the house." [88]

The army asked children from Chichupac if they had seen their mothers helping "people with guns." And the victimization of children goes beyond using them to pressure their parents; in one . . . sweep, 24 of the 28 people "captured" were children. [89]

"One of my brothers . . . was very dedicated to weaving. For example, he had responsibilities in the cooperative.

"In the beginning of November [1980] they came to our house to kidnap my brother. They tortured him terribly. It was especially bad because he had cancer in one foot and could not walk well. Thirty armed men in civilian clothes came and took him, not allowing him to dress. He wore only his underwear . . . not even shoes. This was the rainy season and there was lots of water and mud. They tied him up and shoved him into the puddles and the mud and then they took him before the houses of his friends and relatives, asking 'Do you know this man?' No one could speak because they were frightened. My brother told them, 'Speak my name – don't be afraid.'

"After going past the houses they took him two kilometers away. There are many ravines, very deep ones, around where I lived. There, where a number of trees stood in one of the ravines, they hanged him. They bound his hands outstretched on either side and they thrust a knife into his chest.

"I had photographs of him. A friend took those pictures but I had to leave them in Guatemala. It's too bad I don't have them. But they actually crucified him. They bound him with ropes and pierced him in the chest with a knife. The same, the same as the crucifixion. It was terrible." [90]

cos, March 27 by armed men who entered her house during the night and took her away; she was not allowed to s or put on her shoes • Celita Florinda Lucero, 26, employee of the Adams Factory and union member, disappeared he was going to get her passport renewed, Guatemala City, April 12 • Dora Herminia Santos, 10, and her

By the end of 1980, over 400 teachers had been killed. In 1980 alone, 226 teachers were assassinated, and numbers swelled in 1981. In just one teachers' union local, 35 members were killed in the first six months of 1981. In an average month, 14 teachers are killed.[91]

The majority of the country's schools are totally destroyed or abandoned, due to the authorities' negligence, and Guatemalan children are educated in disheartening conditions, stated the newspaper *El Gráfico* on Feb. 10, 1985. On February 14, the Teacher's Posthumous Aid Society reported that from 1981 to December, 1984, 165 teachers were killed, and 70 were arrested-disappeared.[92]

father disappeared in Zone 4, Guatemala City, April 14 • Violeta Ileana Pérez Sierra, 10, disappeared in Guatemala as she was going to night school, April 23 • Thelma Odilia Cuchijay Reyes, 13, with her 6-year-old brother, going to bread near her home in Zone 11, Guatemala City, were stopped by armed men who, throwing her brother aside,

na in a car and drove away, April 26 • Sandra Jeaneth Morales Pineda, 16, secondary student, disappeared after
ing her home to go to a nearby dispensary in Zone 7, Guatemala City, May 2 • Berta Anabella de Corado disappeared
r having been detained by security police at a checkpoint in Roosevelt Hwy, Zone 11, Guatemala City, May 5 •

"*The army came to an* aldea *near Chimaltenango or Antigua, I'm not exactly sure. But women were weaving when the army arrived. 'What are you doing? Why are you weaving?' And the first thing the soldiers did was to cut down the loom with a machete. And when they had cut down all the warp threads of the loom they began raping two young women. After raping them, they tortured them. They cut off their hands and cut off their noses and ears in front of their own mother. This is what my sister told me. It is terrible what is happening now. Then they asked the mother, 'Can you recognize which is the older?' The mother couldn't answer because she had fainted after seeing what the army had done. This is one of thousands of incidents that have happened in Guatemala.*" [93]

Morelia Villeda Carranza, 18, disappeared after leaving a friend's house in Zone 7, Mixco, Guatemala, May 6 • M. Cristina Coronado Figueroa, 15, and Josefina Alonzo, night school student, disappeared on a walk at 5 p.m., Zor Guatemala City, May 26 • Aura Carlota Ordoñez Veliz, 16, and Ericka Jeaneth Garcia, 14, disappeared while wall

ther in the afternoon, May 29, Zone 1, Guatemala City • Margarita Jiménez, widow, 55, disappeared when going
her house to the civic center, Zone 4, Guatemala City, May 30 • Ilsa Marisol Sosa de la Cruz, high school student,   75
ppeared after leaving the learning center at 6 P.M. in Guatemala City, June 3 • Gloria Mateo Vallecillo, cafe

employee in El Progreso, Jutiapa, disappeared by five heavily armed men who carried her off to an unkn
destination, June 10 • Blanca Estela Gomez Gonzalez, 16, disappeared while going to visit her sister, Zone
Guatemala City in June • Mariana Ajitzip Coyote and daughters, Florinda Maria Yos and Isabel Yos Atzip, detai

ppeared by several heavily armed, unidentified men who raided their home in Saquilla, an aldea of Patzun, altenango, June 18, and then dragged them off in a military jeep to an unknown destination • Brenda Nineth Tec eon, student, 13, disappeared after leaving her home in Zone 7, Guatemala City, June 21 • Jovita Castillo Montufar,

21, and Maria de Castillo, 22 (sister and wife of Carlos Castillo Montufar, disappeared 6/14/85) disappeared June
Guatemala City after having reported to police about Carlos' disappearance • Haydee Archila Hernandez disappear
unspecified circumstances after leaving Sansare, El Progreso, en route to Guatemala City, June 27 • Nora N

"My mother's mother was abandoned by her husband. She was only able to support herself through weaving. She wove designs of large birds, and she had no book from which she took the designs. Before my grandmother died, at around seventy, she made little garments for children and she only charged fifty centavos for a finished one. With this she could buy tomatoes, onions and lime. Working in her field, she planted corn and beans and in this way she didn't have to buy corn. She was happy making these children's garments. People who were about to become godparents bought them for their godchildren."[94]

"In Guatemala, it is not natural that grandmothers bury their grandchildren," repeated an 85-year-old woman whose two teenage grandchildren were murdered.[95]

secretary, disappeared en route to the National Library, Zone 1, Guatemala City, July 8 • Ana Frida Castellanos de Ga
80 disappeared after leaving her workplace, Zone 1, Guatemala City, July 22 • Gloria Elizabeth Reyes de Herrer, 32, s
representative for Las Flores Cemetery, disappeared after leaving home on her way to work, Guatemala City, July

The fabric of daily life in Rabinal has been permanently changed by the repression and its consequences. There are thousands of widows in the municipality and hardly a house that has not lost a family member. Some villages of a few hundred people, such as Purulha, have an estimated 40 widows. People in Rabinal have always been poor but their poverty is now so extreme that economic sacrifices include members of their own families. After the army burned her house, one young widow with five children tearfully explained that she was going to give up her youngest child, saying, "I love her so much; (that's why) I'm going to give her away."[96]

"We place much importance on weaving because the majority of people in Guatemala are indigenous and they wear traditional clothing. But the government tries to discourage people from wearing their traje pico, *through school regulations and other means. And clothing factories do more than anything else."*[97]

"My husband's grandmother had pieces of old weaving which she had kept since she was a child. Once she took out this package and showed me the old cloths, saying, 'These are our designs. I have saved them so that when I die you will have them to use as samples.'"[98]

ia del Carmen Burrion Toj, 20, disappeared after leaving her home in Zone 7, Guatemala City, August 7 • Rita fina Pineda Aldana, nurse, 45, disappeared as she went to have her passport changed, Guatemala City, September 9   81 ia Maribel Perez Sandoval, high school student, disappeared after leaving her home in Mixco, November 18 • Gloria

In May 1982, army soldiers entered the village and took away four men whose names appeared on a list. None has reappeared. In June soldiers returned and, without warning, began shooting at everyone; many villagers fled to nearby *parcelas*. The soldiers burned the village down and destroyed harvested crops and seeds. Survivors, thereafter, lived in hiding near the *parcelas* where they tried to grow corn and beans. In August, a helicopter opened fire and killed the members of five families, 25 persons, while they were working in the *parcelas*. An army patrol returned to the area on December 28, 1982, and opened fire on people they found working in the *parcelas*, killing an 80 year old man and a woman. The soldiers destroyed the cut and unharvested crops. The villagers tried to live off the remaining food supply, but soon, facing starvation, fled to Mexico. It took them eight days, with little or no food, to arrive at the Chajul camp. [99]

"The town where we lived (San Juan Ostuncalco) suffered tremendous repression. We left on the 27th of August [1983]. We left our homes because they warned us that they were going to burn our houses that night and they were going to kidnap us, take us from our homes. So, when we knew that, we left our houses, we went to stay with neighbors so they wouldn't kill us. And that same night we decided to leave, we left for San Marcos. And we walked on foot for four days with the little ones. And really, without money, we suffered, suffered much from hunger." [100]

Santiago Rojas, detained-disappeared by unidentified men along with Hector Ramiro Flores Morales in the U
82 *Nations Park, Amatitlán, Guatemala, December 11 • 1986: Karla Cortez Monge, 8, kidnapped in Guatemala City, Febr*
7 • Brenda Mijano Quiñónez, 15, kidnapped from a Guatemala City bus stop, February 17 • Gloria Leticia Morán de

disappeared in Guatemala City, February 18 • Gloria Esperanza Balá Yax disappeared February 19, Guatemala City •
eranza Tomás González disappeared after leaving home in Guatemala City, February 23 • Maria Eugenia Moneros, 83
kidnapped from her home by 8 armed men driving a brown panel truck, Zone 11, Guatemala City, March 6 • Lilián

"Now people in my town don't think of weaving. Weaving no longer exists in La Estancia. The weavers are dead. Weaving could revive with a new regime. But with what is happening now, how is it possible? We can't begin to teach our children again or to organize a new weaving cooperative. Impossible.

Never! We must wait for a new government to regain our culture, our ideas, our work." [101]

In urban areas, 60% of women do not know how to read or write. In the countryside, illiteracy reaches 90%. [102]

Yolanda Diaz de Melchor, 31, disappeared March 12 after leaving home in Zone 12, Guatemala City • Emilia Hernán Yoc, 60, disappeared Holy Thursday, Guatemala City • Emy Magnolia Ayala Barán, 20, disappeared after leaving ho Guatemala City, March 20 • María Tzampop Cor, kidnapped March 28 at 1 a.m. in village of Cjoaj, San Anto

nango, Quiché • Hada Patricia García López, 14, disappeared Easter Sunday on her way to work in Zone 1,
emala City • Evelyn Yanaida Diaz Castro, 8, kidnapped by a female in Puerto Barrios, Izabal • Ana Dolores Chumil
us, 11, disappeared from school in Guatemala City, April 10 • Tomasa Ramírez de Quintanilla disappeared on her

85

way to market in Guatemala City, April 13 • Olga Marina Paredes Saravía, 50, disappeared in Guatemala City • Je
Mariel Hernández, 8, disappeared en route to the store, Guatemala City, April 15 • Alma Violeta Rivas del Cia
disappeared in Guatemala City, April 18 • Xiomara Valexca Saraccini Ramazini, 17, disappeared after lunch, Guate

The army . . . has learned that, in spite of having killed the men of peasant families, the women have been able to carry on, fulfilling their responsibilities as women. Many of them have managed to find ways to survive in the areas along the border where they have taken refuge. Excellent weavers, they have improvised looms and continue weaving and embroidering their history even though "thread is very expensive and it is more and more difficult to find." However, there are on the other hand areas where the fear of repression has kept women in a constant state of anxiety that upsets all normal activities of daily life.[103]

, April 19 • Carmelia López Ambrosio de Alvarado, 32, disappeared in Guatemala City, April 19 • Velveth Arlin ayo, 15, disappeared on her way to church in Guatemala City, April 20 • Wilson Rojas and daughters Vilma Lisette, 4, Kelly Jeanette, 6, disappeared in Guatemala City, April 22 • Ana Lisette Alvayero, 12, and her sister Filomena

87

The massacre of Olopa was slow death, not the sudden outburst of Panzos.

Olopa is in Chiquimula. It has many small villages around it – El Rodeo, Amatillo, Agua Blanca, El Camalote, Tunoco, Carrizalito. In a two-year period beginning in 1977, one hundred campesino men, fifteen women and forty children have been killed.

On September 9, 1978, the slaughter increased. The *kaibiles*, the counter-insurgency squad from Montreros, Esquipulas, following orders of plantation owners . . . kidnapped eight men from their houses. The bodies were found later, dead from drowning or strangulation.

On September 26, fifteen more people were kidnapped and assassinated. The following day, the auxiliary mayor of Amatillo, Francisco Garcia, went to the justice of the peace of Olopa to ask for help with identifying and burying the bodies. That night he too was kidnapped and assassinated. Families were not able to bury their dead lest they too be exposed to the same fate.

Witnesses say that when the *kaibiles* arrive, they grab children and break their backs over their knees. Women are hanged or strangled. Cornfields and ranchitos are burned, and cattle are driven into the gardens. Any stores of corn, coffee or beans are robbed.

The villages of Zarzal, Piedra Amolar and Amatillo are totally abandoned.[104]

Xiomara Alvayero, 16, disappeared en route to the movies in Mixco, April 27 • Rosa Lorena Escobar López, kidnappe armed men from a public bus in Guatemala City, April 28 • Emma Leticia Bautista Alvarez, 6, disappeared when went out to buy candy, May 1 • Maria Elena Rodas Orellana, 20, industrial engineering student at San Carlos Nat

..., disappeared after getting off a bus coming from Chimaltenango, May 12 • Ana María González de Ruano, 27, ppeared in Guatemala City, June 11 • Ana María de León Chávez, high school student, disappeared June 13 after ing classes at the Commercial Sciences school in Quezaltenango • María Rosaura Cifuentes Nova, 16, kidnapped by

89

three armed men in downtown Guatemala City, July 1; her boyfriend, an army second-lieutenant, was killed on
spot; her body was found later, shot to death • Julia Jeanette Avilez, 24 disappeared July 13 after leaving
Nutritional Recuperation Center in San Juan Sacatepéquez • Marta Judith Ortiz, 15, kidnapped by armed men near

Question: "Who in your family has disappeared?"

Answer: "My father, Rigoberto Morales."

"My brother, Máynor Morales."

"My brother, Otto Raúl Morales."

"My brother, Armando Roberto Morales."

"My uncle, Moisés Morales."

"My uncle, Salomón Morales."

"My aunt, Lilián Aida Morales."

"My aunt, Elizabeth Morales."

"My aunt, Sipriana Ramírez de Morales."

"My cousin, Damaris Marleni Morales."

"My cousin, María Victoria Morales."

"My cousin, Hector Manolo Morales."

"My cousin, Noé Salomón Morales."

"My cousin, Byron Moisés Morales."

"My cousin, Abygail Morales."

"My cousin, Claudia Roxana Morales."[105]

I am from the village of San Francisco, municipality of Nenton, department of Huehuetenango. The soldiers came to look through our villages. They told us then that everything looked fine in our village. They said that we seemed to be happy and working hard.

The soldiers said to us, "Let's see what the government can do for you. Maybe they will send you some fertilizer. We can see by your hard work that there is a lot to do here. We don't want you and your families to become displeased with your work; we don't want you to go with the guerrillas because they are liars. That's why we have come to look out for you. You stay here quietly. We have a lot of work to do."

"Alright," we said to them.

"You are doing magnificently here, but we have to tell you something. The most important thing is that you are here in your houses, and that you don't leave. If people are not in their houses, then we will have to kill them because they are the ones who are ruining Guatemala."

"We don't understand this," we said. "We are working honorably here with our families. We are working to feed ourselves so that our wives and children do not go hungry. We have animals that we are tending here at the *finca* . . ."

"That is good," they said. They came to my house and I gave them coffee; they were satisfied and went off to town.

It was peaceful for two or three days. Then they came back.

"You are living here quietly, but we have to come back to your area again," they said. "Don't be afraid of us, because we are the government army. If you people stay here quietly, you'll be safe."

"Fine," we said. We fed them; they ate what we ate. We even thanked them. Then they left. We knew why they had come — they had come for us, sure.

"Things here are quiet, but we're going to come back. Don't be afraid, don't flee. We are here defending Guatemala for you. The government sent us here for you, to see what was happening here in your villages."

"Well, that's fine, because we are living and working peacefully at home," we said.

Then, they came looking house by house. "Everything seems fine, we hope you stay this quiet. We'll come back another time; don't be afraid." That's what they said when they left. When they came the second time, it was to massacre us.

The army came down to our village at about 11 o'clock in the morning. The clothing they had on was kind of purple; it was *pinto* . . . that's their dress. At about 11:00 the helicopter came to drop off their food, but they came on foot. They all came at the same time; perhaps they had radios and they communicated to each other about what time they would arrive.

The helicopter was plain white. I really didn't get close to it because I was working when I heard the sound of the helicopter coming down there in the field. It landed, but it was on its way up by the time I got there.

I know it was carrying food because some of our *compañeros* went to unload the cargo that had been brought for the army. When the ones who had carried it came back they told us, "We unloaded a lot of food from the helicopter." They took it to the school and piled it up there. We didn't get a chance to see the other things. The *compañeros* said they were very heavy. We heaped it all together at the town hall.

Soon after, they came to the house and called us. They told us to go to the courthouse because the soldiers had to tell us something.

"There is going to be a meeting. The colonel wants to have a discussion with you; go and hear him, and make sure you listen carefully." That's what the soldiers said, according to my wife who told me about it when I got home. So I changed my clothes and went to catch up with the others. Since we did not know what wrong we had done, we did not think that they had come to kill us. The first time, they had told us not to fear them, so by then we had begun to trust the soldiers, even when we got there and were put in the courthouse.

Whoever arrived was taken inside the courthouse.

They separated everyone. They put the men in the courthouse, and the women and children in the Catholic church. The mothers carried their children with them.

When our houses were empty, they went back to look through them and take all of our things. They stole clothes, tape recorders, radios, watches, and money, whatever they could.

Our cooperative in San Francisco had 10,000 *quetzales*. Some villagers kept their money there, also; some had 50, 100, or even up to 1,000 *quetzales*, but the army took it all. Whatever they saw, they stole. We watched them carrying around chickens, eggs, baskets and pots. They were gathering more and more things there on the school patio. They even took all of the tortillas they could find in our houses,

the ones our wives had made.

After they had taken all of our things, they came and asked us for a cow.

"Now we want you to bring two head of cattle for us to eat. We've come here for you, you see; we're going to have a *fiesta* here with you right now." We started realizing then that they were going to kill us.

"Okay, we'll give them to you."

"But you're going to give us cattle that belong to you and not to the *finca*."

"What, we are not shameless. We are hardworking people. We have animals that we've raised ourselves. You can see for yourselves by their markings."

"Well, alright," they said. The cattle arrived and were killed . . . One belonged to Pedro and the other to a man named Andres. The army wanted them for nothing — they didn't pay us. We were afraid because

they carried arms and many of them had bayonets. They are frightening. We didn't know what to do. We are *campesinos*, agriculturalists, laborers — working people.

The soldiers killed and skinned the cattle on the school patio. They ate the meat with the tortillas they'd found in the houses.

When they had finished, they closed the doors of the courthouse, but there were two or three holes in the windows, so we could see outside.

The soldiers took our wives out of the church in groups of ten or twenty. Then twelve or thirteen soldiers went into our houses to rape our wives. After they were finished raping them, they shot our wives and burned the houses down.

All of our children had been left locked up in the church which is about twenty meters from the courthouse . . . they were crying, our poor children were screaming. They were calling us. Some of the bigger ones were aware that their mothers were being killed and were shouting and calling out to us.

They took the children outside. Only the little ones, the 5-, 6-, and 8-year-olds, the 2-year-olds were left together inside the church. The soldiers had already brought out all the mothers and killed them. Then they brought out the babies — two, one and a half, three years old. They were all holding on to each other. The 10-, 12-, 8-, 5- and 6-year-olds were also brought out in groups. The soldiers killed them with knife stabs. We could see them. They killed them in a house in front of the church. They yanked them by the hair and stabbed them in their bellies; then they disemboweled our poor little children. Still they cried. When they finished disemboweling them, they threw them into the house, and then brought out more.

We could see it all. We were very frightened because we realized that we and our families were being murdered. They finished with our poor families and then they set fire to that house, too. It burned right away. They were pouring something, maybe gasoline, on the houses. They had a broom which they used for sweeping the houses when they didn't catch fire easily because of the rain. We watched what they did. They brushed first, then set the fire with a match, and the fire burned fast.

Finally they brought out the last child. He was a little one, maybe two or three years old. They stabbed him and cut out his stomach. The little child was screaming, but because he wasn't dead yet the soldier grabbed a thick, hard stick and bashed his head. They held his feet together and smashed him against a tree trunk. I saw how they flung him hard and hurt his head. It split open, and they threw him inside the house. Then the soldier came over to us, and we couldn't see anymore . . . They came to get us, too. So I didn't see how they finished with all of our families, our children.

Then they started with the old people.

"What fault is it of ours," the old people said. "No sir, we are tired, we aren't thinking anything. It seems we're not good for anything anymore."

"Nothing, not shit, not tired, not . . . OUTSIDE!" a soldier said. They took the poor old people out and stabbed them as if they were animals. It made the soldiers laugh. Poor old people, they were crying and suffering. They killed them with dull machetes. They took them outside and put them on top of a board; then they started to hack at them with a rusty machete. It was pitiful how they broke the poor old people's necks.

"Aaay, aaay," cried the poor old man. They were beheading him. He was the only one they did that to. They brought out the next one and knifed him under the ribs. With one plunge they did it. He did not suffer as much. But the first one suffered a lot because they beheaded him with a dull knife. The knife they were using was all rusted. Later they were given new knives. They stabbed the people in the ribs; they opened a big hole and streams of blood came pouring out . . . that made them laugh. About twelve old people were stabbed to death. Then it was over, and they began shooting us.

They began to take out the adults, the grown men of working age. They took us out by groups of ten. Soldiers were standing there waiting to throw the prisoners down in the patio of the courthouse. Then they shot them. When they finished shooting, they piled them up and other soldiers came and carried the bodies into the church . . . I don't know what they wanted with those poor bodies they put in the church. I only saw them there when I escaped. From a hill I saw the flames coming from the church. They burned them there . . . .[107]

Those killed during the San Francisco Massacre included the following women:

Ana Paíz Domingo
Isabela García Silvestre
Isabela Paíz García
María Paíz García
Angelina Paíz García
Isabela Paíz Paíz
Isabela García Marcos
Isabela Paíz García
María Ramos Paíz
Angelina Paíz Ramos
María Paíz García
Juana Paíz García
Isabela Paíz García
Angelina Paíz García
María Paíz García
María Paíz
Angelina Paíz García
Angelina Perez
María Ramos
María García
María Gomez García
Juana Ramos R.
María Gomez R.
Eulalia Paíz
María Gomez R.
María Gomez R.
Eulalia Marcos M.
Angelina Ramos L.
Juana Ramos M.
Eulalia Paíz
Isabela Domingo
Eulalia Paíz D.
María Paíz
Angelina Paíz
Isabela Domingo
María Paíz
Catarina Pérez Lucas
Ana Ramos
Catarina García Paíz
Ana Ramos García
Juana Ramos García
Angelina Ramos García
Isabel Pérez Ramos
Ana Ramos Pérez
Catarina Ramos Pérez
Juana Lucas Paíz
Eulalia Lucas Paíz
María Ramos
Eulalia Alonso
Juana García Silvestre
María Paíz García
Ana Paíz Ramos

Juana Lucas Paíz
Catarina Ramos
María Paíz Domingo
Catarina Pérez Domingo
Juana Pérez Domingo
Ana Pérez Ramos
Ana Paíz Ramos
Catarina Paíz Ramos
Angelina Paíz Ramos
Juana Paíz García
Catarina Pérez Paíz
Isabel Pérez Paíz
Ana Mendoza
Catarina Pérez Mendoza
Ana Pérez Mendoza
Isabel Pérez
Eulalia Andres
Ana Gómez Andres
María Mendoza
María García Paíz
María Ramos García
María Ramos Mendoza
María Ramos Juan
Isabel Paíz Domingo
Isabela Paíz Domingo
Isabela Lucas
Isabela Ramos L.
Juana Lucas
Isabela García
Catarina Lucas
Ana Silvestre Lucas
Angelina Silvestre Lucas
Isabela Silvestre Lucas
Angelina Santizo
María Ramos
Ana Silvestre Ramos
Angelina Silvestre R.
María Silvestre R.
Isabela Domingo Paíz
Isabela García
Ana Paíz Ramos
Catarina Ramos Lucas
Isabela Paíz García
María Paíz García
Juana Paíz García
Eulalia Sebastian
Catarina Ramos
María Paíz Silvestre
Juana Lucas Lucas
María García Velasco
Petrona Mendoza
Isabela Ramos
Angelina Paíz
Juana Lucas
Magdalena Lucas
María Lucas

Magdalena Lucas Miguel
Catarina Lucas Velasco
Petrona Domingo
María Silvestre
María García Silvestre
Ana Santizo
Petrona García S.
María García S.
Petrona Lucas
María García L.
Catarina García L.
Petrona García L.
María Paíz R.
Eulalia Paíz R.
Isabela García
Magdalena Marcos G.
Juana Marcos G.
Juana Marcos G.
Juana Martín
Isabela Pérez
Juana Marcos R.
María Gomez Andrés
Angelina Marcos
Eulalia Paíz
Angelina Domingo P.
María García
Juana Diego D.
Juana Lucas
Eulalia Ignacio
María Lucas
Angelina Ramos L.
Catarina Ramos L.
Isabela García S.
Catarina García P.
María Lucas G.
Eulalia Paíz
Isabela Paíz
Catarina Paíz
Catarina Lucas R.
María Pérez
Isabela Pérez
María Ignacio P.
Ana García P.
María Pérez R.
Juana Paíz R.
Catarina Paíz R.
Angelina Paíz Silvestre
Isabela Ramos

According to a State Department memo, there are up to 250,000 displaced persons in Guatemala. Other estimates are as high as one million. People who live near Mexico, Honduras or Belize are most likely to seek foreign asylum. Others abandon their villages but remain in the country.[108]

Mexico is a haven for a somewhat smaller number of refugees than the United States, but if the number were calculated in proportion to population, Mexico's ratio is much higher. Moreover, given the respective resources of the two countries, Mexico is bearing a far greater burden than the United States. Yet while the United States has forcibly repatriated tens of thousands of Central American refugees, the number who have been forcibly repatriated from Mexico is much smaller.[109]

It is difficult to offer an accurate assessment of the total number of Guatemalan refugees who have crossed into Mexico. A conservative estimate would be over 150,000. The greatest concentration of refugees is found in the border province of Chiapas. There are about 90,000 Guatemalan refugees in Chiapas and about 60,000 in the rest of the country, including those in Campeche, Mexico City and the floating refugee population travelling north.[110]

The majority of the refugees arrived in Mexico after a long journey through the jungle without adequate food, shelter or clothing. They arrived in Mexico with signs of malnutrition and diseases ranging from internal parasites and dysentery to malaria. Many also had severe psychological problems due to the shocking experiences they underwent in Guatemala. Two to three years after arriving in Mexico, the refugees remain a high risk health group: 25% of the population in the camps is underweight and the infant mortality rate fluctuates around 200 per 1,000.[111]

"What did you do with your houses, your animals, the things that you had? Did you take them, sell them, or leave them there?"

"We couldn't take them; some of us had sheep, others a horse or an ox. We couldn't take them. The things in our houses were left because they weighed a lot. We only could take the clothes we could wear and our blankets. The rest we left behind." [112]

"Why did you leave your land?"

"We left because they threatened us, they told us that at the end of the month they were going to kill all the Indian people, 'All the Inditos,' they told us, and they were 'going to get rid of all the aldeas around.'" [113]

Guatemalan security forces entered San Juan Ixcan on May 15, 1982, and killed whomever they found, burning alive two families in their homes. Those who escaped fled to the mountains and lived off the crops on 88 nearby *parcelas* for about four months. In early September, 1982, army patrols pursued them in the hills and strangled to death four children who were unable to escape. In late September, two helicopters and two planes bombed the *parcelas*, destroying crops and livestock. In early January, 1983, the army and helicopters spent three days in the area, burning the unharvested crops and food supply and killing livestock. Soldiers also shot to death four peasants who had gone to the *parcelas* to cut corn. It took nine days for these 105 persons to reach the refugee camp at Chajul, during which time they had to elude army patrols and constant helicopter surveillance of the area. Many villages and settlements in the municipality of Chajul that they passed during their flight to Mexico, including Kaibil Balam, Santo Tomas, Ilom, Chill, Xaxmoxan and Cagnixla, had been burned and devastated in a manner similar to their own cooperative.[114]

The social chaos in Guatemala [in 1982] is more pervasive than that resulting from the 1976 earthquake, when 20,000 people lost their lives and 200,000 homes were destroyed. Catholic bishops in Guatemala claim that political violence has already destroyed more homes than the earthquake.[115]

"When we were in Chiapas, people told me I had to stop wearing traje. I cried when I put away my traje. When I put on a dress I felt as though I was naked. It wasn't like wearing things you make yourself, that are so comfortable. I didn't want to show myself to my children in a dress. But out of necessity I did it." [116]

"We left, fleeing the gunfire of the army of the government of President Ríos Montt's Guatemala. We slept on the mountainsides. It rained. There was a downpour. Our children slept in our arms, covered with our shirts, because we left without blankets. We had nothing to cover ourselves. The soldiers began by burning our houses; then they came looking for us in the mountains in order to kill us. We fled our camp sites without food, without water, suffering the bites of insects. The following day many children died and some pregnant women gave birth in the mountains. And we had nothing to eat.

"We found a creek. Finally we drank water. The children were crying of hunger. So a few of the men went to look for corn in the fields or granaries. But they ran into soldiers and died seeking something for their children to eat." [117]

"Our culture has survived because it was not made in one month or one year. Rather, it comes from our ancestors. When more than four hundred fifty years ago the Spaniards came to conquer and invade Guatemala, they wanted to destroy our customs, our entire culture, but this was not possible because it is something within our very hearts, it is very deep within us. It is inscribed within us. Our culture and our customs are so deeply rooted within us that they go wherever we go. And now we are struggling for this entire culture. We are fighting for all those things which the rich and the colonels want by stepping on us with all their might. But it is not possible for them to win because we Indians are the majority in the country and when we are united and increase our strength they will not be able to finish us off . . . In reality we are defending our culture, our language, our customs, our religiosity which we understand differently from the way they understand it. What they want is that we go on losing our customs, but we have carried our customs for many years, for hundreds of years, for four hundred fifty years. Ever since the Spaniards arrived in Guatemala they have been trying to destroy our customs but they have not been able to. And they will not be able to because we will keep on respecting all of that which is really ours.

"Even our Indian dress has come under attack in Guatemala because we are obliged to take it off. Why? Because the rich and the army say that all of us Indian people are communists, and subversive. So for our own safety, so that they will not take us, so that they will not kidnap and torture us, we have stopped wearing our Indian dress. This is a painful thing because for us this way of dressing is also our culture . . .

"The government uses us or has used us in the past, when they

"Each town has its custom. When the nixtamal is boiling over the fire you put in the escudilla and that strengthens it. But jarritos chiquitos — small pots we use to take coffee to visit friends — we don't put these trastes over the fire. That way they keep their color. Some trastes we have just for visits to friends, for atole or coffee.

"They had other customs In Mexico. For example, in Guatemala we always kept hot water on the fire all day long; it was there any time we wanted hot water . But in Chiapas everything was different. No hot water on the fire. I thought, 'Here I will lose all my Guatemalan customs.' Finally I found a Guatemalan selling clay trastes in Mexico and once again I had the things I was used to. It is very different to cook atole or rice in other trastes. Now [in the U.S.] I miss my trastes."[118]

thought it was in their interest. They exhibited us in our native dress as if we were in a zoological park where people would come and pay them money to see us. But now they have us as their worst enemy. They have exhibitions in their Clubs where they drink, dance, and bring their foreign friends. They exhibit our clothes and with all this, without any effort of their own, they rake in money – by showing things we make, our pots in which we cook our beans, the ceramics and earthenware which we use, our huipiles which we weave.

And to enter this exhibit costs a lot of money. So in this way the government has used us, but now we are no longer lending ourselves to these games. Now, we have realized that instead of weaving another huipil, we are better off picking up a weapon, picking up a bomb and throwing it in front of them.

"I do not think of myself as a terrorist or a subversive because what I am doing is struggling so that our children can have a good education, housing and food, like the rich have. It's for this that we are fighting. I am not a terrorist because I will never take up a weapon and kill a person who has done nothing to me, like they do. So to the contrary, I think the government and its army – they are the terrorists because they take up their weapons, their tanks, their mortars, their airplanes and go out and massacre entire villages and all the people who stand in their way. They come to bomb. This is terrorism. By contrast I am fighting for peace, for justice, and for the liberation of my people."[119]

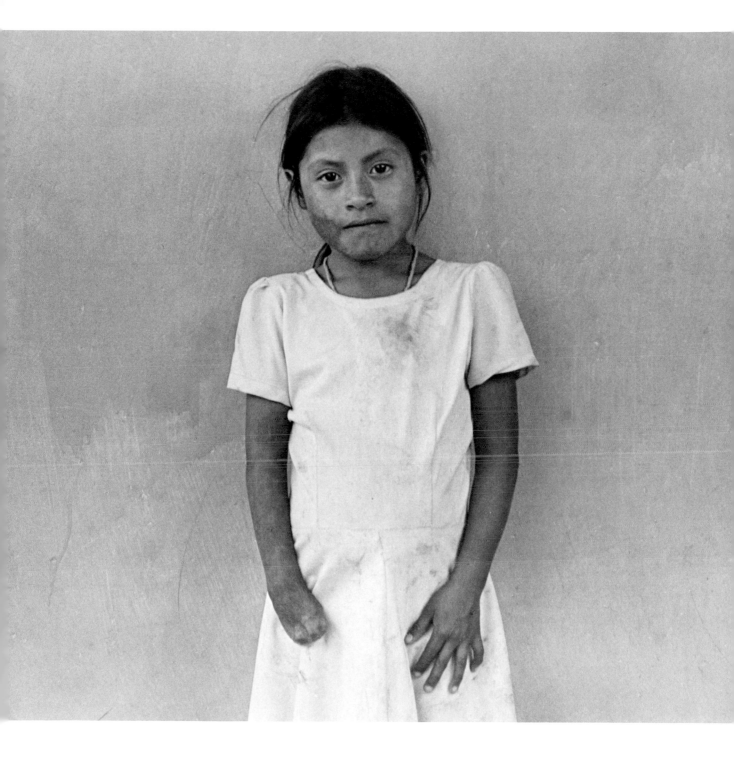

De pie, cantar
que vamos a triunfar
avanzan ya
banderas de unidad
y tú vendras
marchando junto a mí

De pie, luchar
el pueblo va a triunfar
será mejor
la vida que vendrá
a conquistar
nuestra felicidad.

Stand up, sing
we are going to win.
Flags of unity
are advancing now
and you will come
marching together with me.

Stand up, struggle,
the people will win.
It will be better
the life that will come
to win
our happiness.[120]

"In most of the refugee camps in Chiapas, women are making an effort to continue weaving, though not the same designs they did in Guatemala. They are doing this out of necessity, for they now have many needs. And they must complete their weaving as quickly as possible to support their families.

"Even though our designs are not the same, the act of weaving represents something very important. It shows people on the outside that we want to live, we don't want to die.

"I don't want to stop participating in my culture. I teach people about this craft that the whole world admires – so simple and beautiful. Too often, our art was never appreciated as it should have been in Guatemala.[121]

"Through solidarity we send the message of a suffering people – a message of the pain, the sadness, the terror which the people of Guatemala, especially Indian people, experience. There isn't anyone they can turn to. Their own government wants to be rid of them and wants to have their lands, lands that were their Mayan ancestors'. When the Spaniards realized there was no gold in Guatemala they began to steal that land. And now these landowners are great exporters of cotton, coffee, beef, cardamon. And here are we, begging in other countries to live, while they – the rich – get richer every day at the cost of the blood and hunger of the people. This is what is happening in Guatemala."[122]

AFTERWORD
by Margarita and Thomas Melville

Granddaughters of Corn makes a unique contribution to the literature, to the art, to the information on Guatemala. Many of the facts contained herein have been published elsewhere, by Amnesty International, by America's Watch, by the Human Rights Commission of the OAS, and by numerous works written by committed authors. The photographs, however, are originals. Originals in style, originals in composition, and originals in content. But neither the photographs nor the text are why we consider this such an important work. It is the juxtaposition of the two, the serenic scenes of beautiful women and their daughters looking confidently into the camera, and the text which contains descriptions of such incredible cruelty against the poor and the powerless, especially its Indian women, who are represented by those in the photographs.

Why put such text and photos together? It seems almost a parody to put such beauty in the midst of such ugliness. But it is not a parody because this is Guatemala, wherein unsurpassed beauty and uncomprehensible ugliness come together in a way that forces the knowing observer to question the very nature of humankind.

But this book is not a philosophical treatise intended to ask, let alone answer, probing questions on the nature and motivations of despicable human activities. It is a book intended to be left on middle class coffee tables where unsuspecting guests can pick it up and thumb through it. Attracted by the pristine beauty of the subjects in the photos, the text will be perused and a sense of incredulity will result. The reader will gradually realize that he/she has been seduced into looking at the reality of Guatemala in a way that tourists never do, in a way that the Guatemalan elite would prohibit if it had the power, in a way that the U.S. government blatantly denies and hopes that its citizens never believe.

Having gotten beyond a key obstacle that all historiographers of the Guatemalan scene confront, that is, capturing an audience's attention long enough to lead them beyond their ethnocentric biases to see the social forces at work in Guatemala, the author's confront the major problem: how does one make the events recounted in the text believable?

None of us doubt that what happened to the Jews in Nazi Germany was an historical tragedy. We do not understand how or why it happened but we know that it did happen. We have seen the photographs of the piles of grotesque corpses, we have seen the ovens where the crimes took place, we have seen the perpetrators tried and sentenced. We try to explain to ourselves that Hitler was a madman, the cause of such destruction and death, and madmen appear on the stage of history from time to time. But Hitler's supposed madness does not explain the complicity of the German and Austrian peoples in his crimes. Hitler was followed into madness by an entire generation of his countrymen, many of whom today continue to deny any guilt.

But we are tempted to think, Nazi Germany was a one-time event for modern man. Or was it? We have also heard of Josef Stalin, of Idi Amin, of Pol Pot. But we explain their unspeakable crimes as the product of communism, or of Africanism, or of Orientalism, that somehow these people and their cohorts are made from different matter than ourselves, or that somehow modern culture has not caught up with them. These are the contemporary versions of ancient racism and ethnocentric doctrines. We cannot imagine ourselves participating in anything so barbaric, so evil, so inhuman. *Granddaughters of Corn* is meant to tell us that there is a regime in Guatemala today like those of Idi Amin, of Pol Pot, of Josef Stalin and of Adolf Hitler and it was put in place and is kept there by the United States of America.

Most United States citizens will recoil at that thought. The authors first ask their readers to believe that the facts detailed in their text are true and verifiable and now we are asking you to accept the complicity of the government of the United States in those atrocities. Further, might we not ask you to believe that the country that does much of the training of Guatemala's counterinsurgency troops, that arms them, that set up the electronic system for detecting all reunions not sanctioned by the government, that has developed a system of thought control and quasi-prison camps called "model villages" is none other than Israel, the home of these same Jewish people whom Hitler tried to exterminate and who still insist we must never forget what he did? Israel and the United States and Guatemala are showing us that we are all of one human nature, treading a fine line between beauty and ugliness, between sanity and madness, between goodness and evil. Why do some of us go in one direction and others in the opposite direction? It is a question that all of us must continuously ask ourselves. If Guatemalan citizens can be so savage and brutal toward the beauty that their nation has produced, let us all take warning of the turbulent forces bottled up within us.

Granddaughters of Corn is the story of a people caught in beauty and tragedy, but let us not think that it is only their story. It is ours as well.

— Pinole, CA
March, 1987

114

Notes:

1. These lines are from the song, "desapariciones" by Ruben Blades, from his album *Buscando America* (Elektra/Asylum Records, New York, 1983). The original is in Spanish:
   ¿Adonde van los desaparecidos?
   Busca en el agua y en los matorrales.
   ¿Y por qué es que se desaparecen?
   Porque no todos somos iguales.
   ¿Y cuando vuelven el desaparecido?
   Cada vez que los trae el pensamiento.
2. Ximena Bunster-Burotto argues that, with local and regional variations, the systematic abuse of women is endemic to Latin America. "Surviving Beyond Fear: Women and Torture in Latin America," *Women and Change in Latin America,* edited by June Nash and Helen Safa, (Bergin & Garvey, South Hadley, Massachusetts; 1986).
3. Women for Guatemala, *The Truth About Guatemalan Women,* (Washington, n.d. [1983?]), p. 10
4. Amnesty International, *"Disappearances" in Guatemala under the Government of General Oscar Humberto Mejía Victores (August 1983 - January 1985),* (New York, 1985), p.1
5. Women for Guatemala, *The Truth About Guatemalan Women,* (Washington, n.d. [1983?]), p. 12
6. Americas Watch Committee, *Guatemala: A Nation of Prisoners,* (New York, 1984) pp. 110-111
7. Grupo de Apoyo Mutuo por el Aparecimiento con vida de Nuestros Familiares: Mutual Support Group for the Appearance of our Relatives Alive.
8. Stephen Schlesinger and Stephen Kinzer, *Bitter Fruit: The Untold Story of the American Coup in Guatemala* (Anchor Books, Garden City, New York; 1983); Susanne Jonas and David Tobis, editors, *Guatemala: "And sovictory is born Even in the bitterest hours,"* North American Congress on Latin America, (New York, 1974).
9. Unidad Revolucionaria Nacional de Guatemala: Guatemalan National Revolutionary Unity.
10. Shelton H. Davis and Julie Hodson, *Witness to Political Violence in Guatemala: The Suppression of a Rural Development Movement,* [Oxfam America], (Boston, 1982), p. 15
11. Iglesia Guatemalteca en el Exilio, "Así es nuestra Historia", *Informe Especial,* 2 (Feb-Mar, 1984), p. 19
12. "Health: The Right of Everyone," *Ch' Abuj Ri Ixoc* [The Voice of the Women], III, 1 (Winter, 1985), p. 7
13. These are lines from the poem by Salvadoran poet Roque Dalton, "O.E.A."
   ["O.A.S." — Organization of American States]. The original is:
   Y el Presidente de los Estados Unidos es más Presidente de mi país
   que el Presidente de mi país
14. *Nunca Más: The Report of the Argentine National Commission of the Disappeared,* Farrar Straus Giroux (New York, 1986). *Torture in Brazil: A Report by the Archdiocese of Sao Paolo,* Vintage Books (New York, 1986).
15. *Nunca Más,* p. 442; *Torture in Brazil,* p. 61.
16. It is impossible to resist drawing parallels between the invocation of national security by Argentine and Brazilian— not to mention Guatemalan — military personnel and the assertions of Lieutenant-Colonel North and Admiral Poindexter that national security interests justified their subversion of the Constitution of the United States. One can only speculate on the procedures for detaining persons incorporated into North's martial law plan, to be implemented following outright suspension of the constitution!
17. Pastoral letter of the Guatemalan Bishops Conference, October, 1985. Cited in *Enfoprensa,* 10/18/85.
18. *Guatemala Revised: How the Reagan Administration Finds "Improvements" in Human Rights in Guatemala,* Americas Watch (New York, 1985).
19. *Enfoprensa,* 3-43 (Nov. 29, 1985), p. 3
20. *Enfoprensa,* 3-24 (June 28, 1985), p. 3
21. These lines, translated by Jonathan Garlock, are from the poem "Oracion Por El Alma De La Patria," [Prayer for the Soul of My Country] by Otto René Castillo, *Informe de Una Injusticia,* EDUCA (San José, 1982):

   Hundo mis manos en la tierra
   y las semillas se me escapan
   como ágiles lágrimas del campo.
   . . .
   Hundo mi corazón en medio de la tierra
   y por las milpas despliego sus hazañas
   cuando crece pleno de cortesías
   cereales . . .
   . . .

Amemos, sin embargo,
campesinos callados de mi patria,
dioses multiplicados por el hambre,
vocativos ejemplos de la hoguera maya
amemos, a pesar de todo,
la redonda emoción de nuestro barro,
porque mañana, campesinos mayas,
nietos del maíz, abuelos de mis manos
la pureza perfumada de la tierra
será para vosotros

22. This documentation project was sponsored, in part, by an award from the Services to the Field program of the National Endowment for the Arts. Prior to these trips, Marilyn had lived and worked in Guatemala on several occasions since her first stay in 1965.
23. *Enfoprensa,* 3-16 (May 3, 1985), p. 4
24. Edelberto Torres-Rivas, "Guatemala — Crisis and Political Violence," *NACLA Report on the Americas,* XIV, 1 (Jan.-Feb. 1980), pp. 20
25. *Enfoprensa,* 3-16 (May 3, 1985), p. 4
26. Watson Guptill (New York, 1978).
27. At the request of a refugee assistance group, we brought some twenty of these drawings back to the United States. Several of them were subsequently included in the traveling exhibit, "Guatemala: A Testimony," sponsored by the Guatemalan Relief Project. Some were also used in the film, *When the Mountains Tremble.*
28. Authors' interview with a refugee women's group, Mexico City, September, 1987.
29. Edelberto Torres-Rivas, "Guatemala — Crisis and Political Violence," *NACLA Report on the Americas,* XIV, 1 (Jan.-Feb. 1980), pp. 20-21
30. Ricardo Falla, "El Hambre y Otras Privaciones Inducidas por el Ejercito de Guatemala sobre la Poblacion Civil," [Hunger and Other Privations Induced by the Guatemalan Army Among the Civilian Population], Iglesia Guatemalteca en el Exilio, *Edicion Especial,* (Sept, 1983), p.42
31. Americas Watch Committee, *Guatemala: A Nation of Prisoners,* (New York, 1984), p. 159, citing *La Razon,* Oct. 3 [1983?]
32. These lines are from Traven's novel, *General from the Jungle,* (Hill & Wang; New York, 1974). They are spoken by the commander of a force sent to subdue a rebellion of enslaved mahogony workers, nearly all Indians, in southern Mexico. The rebellion and its cause are the subject of this and five other works which together comprise Traven's "jungle novels." They offer a vivid account of the peonage system through which labor has been extracted from indigenous people in the region.
33. Staff of the Guatemalan Human Rights Commission in Mexico, reviewing these figures gathered by the authors from many sources, commented (September, 1987) that they were conservative.
34. James Painter, *Guatemala: False Hope, False Freedom. The Rich, the Poor and the Christian Democrats.* Catholic Institute for International Relations and Latin America Bureau (Research and Action) Limited (London, 1987), p. 92
35. Authors' interview with member of the Guatemalan Human Rights Commission staff, Mexico City, September, 1987.
36. Authors' interview with participant in refugee weaving project, Chiapas, Mexico, September, 1987.
37. These quotes are respectively from:Victor Perera, *Rites: A Guatemalan Boyhood,* Harcourt, Brace, Jovanovich [New York, 1986], p. 120; and Noa Kleinman, "Women in Guatemala: An Interview with Marta Gloria Torres," (1984). Distributed by the Women's Committee of the Organization in Solidarity with Guatemala (OSGUA), n.p.
38. *Enfoprensa,* 3-14 (Apr 19, 1985), p. 2
39. Lilly de Jongh Osborne, *Indian Crafts of Guatemala and El Salvador,* [University of Oklahoma Press], (Norman, 1965), p. 94
40. George Black, "Under the Gun," *NACLA Report on the Americas,* (Nov-Dec 1985), p. 16
41. Sources of information on communities attacked by the army include the following: "Massacres: Guatemala, 1978-1984," list compiled by Women for Guatemala (n.d.); "Guatemala: Masacres Cometidas por el Ejercito, 1981-1985" [Guatemala: Massacres Committed by the Army, 1981-1985], annotated map published by Iglesia Guatemalteca en el Exilio (n.d.); Chris Krueger and Kjell Enge, *Security and Development Conditions in the Guatemalan Highlands,* Washington Office on Latin America, (Washington, 1985) — especially Table 1, "Summary of Municipal Data on Effects of Violence," pp. 6-10
42. Amnesty International, *"Disappearances" in Guatemala under the Government of General Oscar Humberto Mejía Victores (August 1983 - January 1985),* (New York, 1985), p.1
43. *Enfoprensa,* 3-30 (August 9, 1985), p.4

44. Souces for information on women who have disappeared include the following: (for 1983-85) Women for Guatemala collations from data published by the Guatemala Human Rights Commission, Amnesty International, and Ixquic; (for 1986) Americas Watch Committee, *Guatemala News in Brief*.
45. Americas Watch Committee, *Guatemala: The Group for Mutual Support, 1984-1985,* (New York, 1985), p.57
46. Ibid, p.3
47. "Sept. 15: No Independence for Majority," *Ch' Abuj Ri Ixoc* [The Voice of the Women], 2-3 (Summer, 1984), p.11
48. Guatemala News and Information Bureau, *Guatemala: The Compañeras Speak,* (n.d.), n.p.
49. *Enfoprensa,* 3-19 (May 24, 1985), p.2
50. Iglesia Guatemalteca en el Exilio, "Así es nuestra Historia", *Informe Especial,* 2 (Feb-Mar, 1984), p.9
51. *Enfoprensa,* 3-14 (Apr, 1985), p.5
52. Tracy Bachrach Ehlers, "Report to the Membership," *Guatemala Scholars Network News,* (Fall, 1985), p.4
53. Comité pro Justicia y Paz de Guatemala, *"Las Desapariciones Forzadas o Involuntarias en Guatemala"* [Forced or Involuntary Disappearances in Guatemala], (Guatemala, 1984), n.p.
54. "Economic Marginization of Women," *Ch' Abuj Ri Ixoc* [The Voice of the Women], III, 2 (Spring, 1985), p.11
55. Authors' interview with Elena Ixcot — a Guatemalan refugee in sanctuary in Weston, Vermont — Oct, 1984
56. Americas Watch Committee, *Guatemala: The Group for Mutual Support, 1984-1985,* (New York, 1985), p.7
57. Noa Kleinman, "Women in Guatemala: An Interview with Marta Gloria Torres," (1984). Distributed by the Women's Committee of the Organization in Solidarity with Guatemala (OSGUA), n.p.
58. Authors' interview with Elena Ixcot — a Guatemalan refugee in sanctuary in Weston, Vermont — Oct, 1984
59. Women for Guatemala, *The Truth About Guatemalan Women,* (Washington, n.d. [1983?]), p.10
60. Ibid, p.4
61. Ibid, p.6
62. Authors' interview with Elena Ixcot — a Guatemalan refugee in sanctuary in Weston, Vermont — Oct, 1984
63. Americas Watch Committee, *Guatemala: The Group for Mutual Support, 1984-1985,* (New York, 1985), p.8
64. Four Arrows, *Guatemala! The Horror and the Hope,* Part One (York, n.d. [1982?]), p.71
65. "Struggle of the Guatemalan Family," *Ch' Abuj Ri Ixoc* [The Voice of the Women], II, 4 (Fall, 1984), p.13
66. Americas Watch Committee, *Guatemala: A Nation of Prisoners,* (New York, 1984), p.211
67. Four Arrows, *Guatemala! The Horror and the Hope,* Part One (York, n.d. [1982?]), p.39
68. *Enfoprensa,* 2-24 (June 15, 1984), p.5
69. Americas Watch Committee, *Guatemala: A Nation of Prisoners,* (New York, 1984), p.108
70. Comité pro Justicia y Paz de Guatemala, *"Human Rights in Guatemala: Summary,* (Feb, 1985), p.15
71. Women for Guatemala, *Guatemala History Told by Its Women,* [transcribed from testimony before the People's Permanent Tribunal, Madrid, Jan 27-30, 1983], Washington, n.d.), p.3
72. Guatemala Human Rights Commission/USA, *Information Bulletin,* III, 10 (Nov-Dec, 1985), p.4
73. Americas Watch Committee, *Guatemala: A Nation of Prisoners,* (New York, 1984), pp.212-3
74. Authors' interview with Efrain Marroquin — a Guatemalan refugee in the U.S. — Nov, 1982
75. Four Arrows, *Guatemala! The Horror and the Hope,* Part One (York, n.d. [1982?]), p.57
76. Comité pro Justicia y Paz de Guatemala, *"Human Rights in Guatemala: Summary,* (Feb, 1985), p.14
77. Four Arrows, "Guatemala! The Terrible Repression and Its Roots in the U.S. National Security State," *Green Revolution,* v.37, no.5 (Late Winter, 1981), p.11
78. Americas Watch Committee, *Guatemala Revised: How the Reagan Administration Finds "Improvements" in Human Rights in Guatemala,* (New York, 1985), p.11
79. "Health: The Right of Everyone," *Ch' Abuj Ri Ixoc* [The Voice of the Women], III, 1 (Winter, 1985), p.2
80. *Enfoprensa,* 3-7 (Feb 22, 1985), p. 5
81. NISGUA, *Guatemala Network News,* III, 6 (Feb/Mar, 1985), p.9
82. Americas Watch Committee, *Guatemala: A Nation of Prisoners,* (New York, 1984), p.132, quoting editorial in *Impacto,* 15 Oct, 1983
83. Iglesia Guatemalteca en el Exilio, "Así es nuestra Historia", *Informe Especial,* 2 (Feb-Mar, 1984), p.29
84. Americas Watch Committee, *Guatemala: A Nation of Prisoners,* (New York, 1984), p.108
85. Iglesia Guatemalteca en el Exilio, "Genocidia en Guatemala," *Boletin,* 14 (Sept, 1982), p.7
86. NISGUA, *Guatemala Network News,* III, 6 (Feb/Mar, 1985), p.9
87. Ibid.
88. Authors' interview with Elena Ixcot — a Guatemalan refugee in sanctuary in Weston, Vermont — Oct, 1984
89. Americas Watch Committee, *Guatemala: A Nation of Prisoners,* (New York, 1984), p.110
90. Authors' interview with Efrain Marroquin — a Guatemalan refugee in the U.S. — Nov, 1982
91. Four Arrows, *Guatemala! The Horror and the Hope,* Part Two (York, n.d. [1982?]), p.134
92. *Enfoprensa,* 3-8 (Mar 1, 1985), p.6
93. Authors' interview with Elena Ixcot — a Guatemalan refugee in sanctuary in Weston, Vermont — Oct, 1984
94. Ibid.

95. Women for Guatemala, *Guatemala History Told by Its Women,* [transcribed from testimony before the People's Permanent Tribunal, Madrid, Jan 27-30, 1983], (Washington, n.d.), p.3

96. Americas Watch Committee, *Guatemala: A Nation of Prisoners,* (New York, 1984), pp.116-17

97. Authors' interview with Efrain Marroquin — a Guatemalan refugee in the U.S. — Nov, 1982

98. Authors' interview with Elena Ixcot — a Guatemalan refugee in sanctuary in Weston, Vermont — Oct, 1984

99. Statement of a young man from San Antonio Tzaga, San Miguel, El Quiche — recorded in Chajul refugee camp, Mar, 1983. Americas Watch Committee, *Guatemalan Refugees in Mexico, 1980-1984,* (New York, 1984), p.91

100. Americas Watch Committee, *Guatemalan Refugees in Mexico, 1980-1984.* (New York, 1984) p. 92

101. Authors' interview with Efrain Marroquin — a Guatemalan refugee in the U.S. — Nov, 1982

102. Ixquic, *Ixquic, The Woman in Guatemala,* (n.d. [1985?]), n.p.

103. Women for Guatemala, *Guatemala History Told by Its Women,* [transcribed from testimony before the People's Permanent Tribunal, Madrid, Jan 27-30, 1983], Washington, n.d.), p.19

104. Four Arrows, *Guatemala! The Horror and the Hope,* Part One (York, n.d. [1982?]), p.40

105. Americas Watch Committee, *Guatemala: The Group for Mutual Support, 1984-1985,* (New York, 1985), n.p.

106. Authors' interview with spokesman of a Guatemalan refugee camp in Mexico — Chiapas, Apr. 1983. His remarks may be translated as follows: "Oh Lord! Defenseless peasants! Folk who have no weapons other than the thankless hoe with which to work the soil! This man (Reagan), so very great, gives arms so that they may kill us all. Such injustice!"

107. Cultural Survival, Inc. and Anthropology Resource Center, *Voices of the Survivors: The Massacre at Finca San Francisco, Guatemala, (Report* 10; Sept, 1983), pp.34-37

108. "Death & Disorder in Guatemala," *Cultural Survival Quarterly,* VII, 1 (Spring, 1983), p.42

109. Americas Watch Committee, *Guatemalan Refugees in Mexico, 1980-1984,* (New York, 1984), pp.1-2

110. Ibid, p.19

111. Ibid, p.21

112. Iglesia Guatemalteca en el Exilio, "Genocidia en Guatemala," *Boletin,* 14 (Sept, 1982), p.8

113. Ibid, p.6

114. Americas Watch Committee, *Guatemalan Refugees in Mexico, 1980-1984,* (New York, 1984), p.90

115. Beatriz Manz, "Guatemalan Refugees: Violence, Displacement, and Survival," *Cultural Survival Quarterly,* VII, 1 (Spring, 1983), p.42

116. Authors' interview with Elena Ixcot — a Guatemalan refugee in sanctuary in Weston, Vermont — Oct, 1984

117. Ricardo Falla, "El Hambre y Otras Privaciones Inducidas por el Ejercito de Guatemala sobre la Poblacion Civil," [Hunger and Other Privations Induced by the Guatemalan Army Among the Civilian Population], Iglesia Guatemalteca en el Exilio, *Edicion Especial,* (Sept, 1983), p.42

118. Authors' interview with Elena Ixcot — a Guatemalan refugee in sanctuary in Weston, Vermont — Oct, 1984

119. Jonathan L. Fried *et al* (eds.), *Guatemala in Rebellion: Unfinished History,* [Grove Press] (New York, 1983), pp. 286-87

120. During a stay in a remote Guatemalan mountain village in 1980 we were awakened late at night by youths singing these lines. They are stanzas of a song born of the popular struggle of Allende's Chile, *El Pueblo Unido Jamas Será Vencido* [A People United Will Never Be Defeated].

121. Authors' interview with Elena Ixcot — a Guatemalan refugee in sanctuary in Weston, Vermont — Oct, 1984

122. Ibid.

Captions:

Glossary:

aldea	Outlying village or hamlet of a larger community; political subdivision of a *municipio*
atole	A nourishing drink made from ground corn
cadejo	Malevolent spirit
comal	Round clay griddle placed directly over the fire for baking tortillas
compañera, compañero	Comrade, friend, mate
copal	[Sp.] Tree resin made into small round cakes used by Mayan Indians as incense for religious rites
corte	Lengths of treadle-loom woven cloth worn by Indian women as skirts
departamento	Political unit of territory headed by a governor. Guatemala has 22 departments or states
desaparecida, desaparecido	A person who has been disappeared
destacamento	Military post
ejido	Communal landholding
escudilla	Soup bowl
finca	Plantation where cash crops such as coffee, cotton, cattle, etc. are grown or raised
GAM	Grupo de Apoyo Mutuo por el Aparecimiento con Vida de Nuestros Familiares — Mutual Support Group for the Appearance of our Relatives Alive
huipil	Upper garment worn by Indian women, generally made of lengths of hand-woven cloth which are decorated with traditional designs and sewn together
indito	Derogatory word for an indigenous Guatemalan
jarrito	Small clay pitcher
kaibiles	Members of a special military force of the Guatemalan army, known for its brutality
ladina, ladino	A person of mixed Spanish/Indian background — literally, *Latinized*
mercado	Marketplace; in rural communities, permanent locations where buying and selling occurs on designated days
municipio	Political unit roughly equivalent to a county (U.S.); *departamentos* consist of *municipios*
nixtamal	Ground corn used for *atole* or, as a dough, for tortillas
parcela	A small plot of land
pinto	Name applied to Guatemalan soldiers wearing camouflage uniforms; also, such uniform itself
pom	[Mayan] Indigenous word for *copal*
quetzal	The national bird of Guatemala, symbol of freedom; said to die in captivity and now in danger of extinction. Also the basic unit of national currency
quintal	Unit of weight: 100 pounds
sahorin	Shaman
tapete	Generally, a woven rug or fiber mat, usually used as a floor covering but also, as in this instance, to cover the ceiling
traje tipico	Traditional garments worn by Indian people
trastes	Kitchen utensils, especially cooking vessels

Selected readings
on human rights, violence and struggle in Guatemala:

Albizures, Miguel Angel. *Tiempo de sudor y lucha.* Praxis Gráfica Editorial. (México, 1987)

Americas Watch Committee. *Guatemala: A Nation of Prisoners.* (New York, 1984)
    Guatemalan Refugees in Mexico, 1980-1984. (New York, 1984)
    Guatemala Revised: How the Reagan Administration Finds "Improvements" in Human Rights in Guatemala. (New York, 1985)
    Guatemala: The Group for Mutual Support, 1984-1985. (New York, 1985)
    Civil Patrols in Guatemala. (New York, 1986)

Americas Watch Committee and British Parliamentary Human Rights Group. *Human Rights in Guatemala during President Cerezo's First Year.* (New York, 1987)

Amnesty International, USA. *"Disappearances" in Guatemala under the Government of General Oscar Humberto Mejía Victores (August 1983-January 1985).* (New York, 1985)

Amnesty International, England. *Guatemala: The Human Rights Record.* (London, 1987)

Andersen, Nicolas. *Guatemala, Escuela Revolucionaria de Nuevos Hombres: Con el Ejército Guerrillero de los Pobres, 1981-1982, Experiencias, testimonios y reflexiones.* Editorial Nuestro Tiempo (Mexico, D.F., 1982)

Anderson, Marilyn. "Guatemala: Traditional Weaving in a Life and Death Struggle." *Craft International* (October-December, 1983)

Benton, Beth. *On the Road to Democracy? A Chronology on Human Rights and U.S.-Guatemalan Relations, January 1978-April 1985.* Central American Historical Institute (Washington, 1985)

Black, George. *Garrison Guatemala.* Monthly Review Press (New York, 1984)

British Parliamentary Human Rights Group. *Bitter and Cruel . . .* (London, 1985)

Castillo, Otto René. *Let's Go!* (Margaret Randall, trans.), Curbstone Press (Willimantic, 1984)
    Tomorrow Triumphant. (Magaly Fernandez and David Volpendesta, eds.), Night Horn Books (San Francisco, 1984)

Clay, Jason (ed.). "Death and Disorder in Guatemala," a collection of articles in *Cultural Survival Quarterly,* Vol. 7, No. 1 (1983)

Comisión de Derechos Humanos de Guatemala. *Guatemala: Ejecuciones Extrajudiciales Colectivas, enero 1981-julio 1985.* (Guatemala, 1985)
    Monthly Report: Human Rights Violations in Guatemala.
    Informe para la Subcomisión de Prevención de Discriminación y Protección de Minorias. ([Guatemala], 1987)

Comité pro Justicia y Paz de Guatemala. *Las Desaparaciones Forzadas o Involuntarias en Guatemala.* (Guatemala, 1984)
    Summary of the Report on the Human Rights Situation in Guatemala (November 1984-October 1985). (Guatemala, 1985)

Concerned Guatemalan Scholars. *Guatemala: Dare to Struggle, Dare to Win.* (Brooklyn, 1982)

Cultural Survival, Inc. and Anthropology Resource Center. *Voices of the Survivors: The Massacre at Finca San Francisco, Guatemala.* (Cambridge, 1983)

Davis, Shelton H. and Julie Hodson. *Witness to Political Violence in Guatemala: The Suppression of a Rural Development Movement.* Oxfam America (Boston, 1982)

Diocesis de San Cristóbal de las Casas, Chiapas, Mexico. *Caminante,* published bi-monthly.

Enfoprensa. *Information on Guatemala.* (Washington), published weekly.

Federación Editorial Mexicana. *Informe de Un Genocidio — los refugiados guatemaltecos.* (Mexico, D.F., 1982)

Four Arrows. *Guatemala! The Horror and the Hope* — Parts One-Four. (York, n.d.)
    "Guatemala! The Terrible Repression and Its Roots in the U.S. National Security State." *Green Revolution,* Vol. 37, No. 5 (Late Winter, 1981)

Frank, Luisa and Philip Wheaton. *Indian Guatemala: Path to Liberation.* EPICA Task Force (Washington, 1984)

Fried, Jonathan *et al* (eds.). *Guatemala in Rebellion.* Grove Press (New York, 1983)

Guatemala Human Rights Commission. *Report on the Situation of Human Rights in Guatemala, 40th UN General Assembly.* (New York, November 1985)
    Guatemalan children today. (México, D.F., September, 1986)

Handy, Jim. *Gift of the Devil: A History of Guatemala.* South End Press (Boston, 1984)

Iglesia Guatemalteca en el Exilio. *Boletín,* published at intervals (Managua)
    Nosotros Conocemos Nuestra Historia. (México, D.F., 1987)

Jonas, Susanne and David Tobias (eds.). *Guatemala: And so victory is born even in the bitterest hours.* NACLA (New York, 1974)

Jonas, Susanne Ed McCaughan and Elizabeth Sutherland Martinez. *Guatemala, Tyranny on Trial: Testimony of the Permanent People's Tribunal.* Synthesis Publications (San Francisco, 1984)

Krueger, Chris and Kjell Enge. *Security and Development Conditions in the Guatemalan Highlands.* Washington Office on Latin America (Washington, 1985)

Macleod, Morna. *GAM-COMRADES: un analisis comparativo.* Ciencia y Tecnologia para Guatemala [CITGUA], *Cuadernos* No. 12 (diciembre, 1986)

Manz, Beatriz. *Guatemala: Cambios en la Comunidad, Desplazamientos y Repatriación.* Editorial Praxis (Mexico, 1987)

Maslow, Jonathan Evan. *Bird of Life, Bird of Death: A Naturalist's Journey Through a Land of Political Turmoil.* Simon and Schuster (New York, 1986)

McClintock, Michael. *The American Connection, Volume Two: State Terror and Popular Resistance in Guatemala.* Zed Books (London, 1985)

Melville, Thomas and Marjorie. *Guatemala: The Politics of Land Ownership.* The Free Press (New York, 1971)

Menchu, Rigoberta. *I...Rigoberta Menchu: An Indian Woman in Guatemala.* Verso (London, 1984)

Montejo, Victor. *Testimony: Death of a Guatemalan Village.* (Victor Perera, trans.) Curbstone Press (Willimantic, 1987)

Monterroso, Jorge E. *Tortura y legalidad en Guatemala.* Ciencia y Tecnologia para Guatemala [CITGUA], *Cuadernos* no. 10 (junio, 1986)

National Lawyers Guild. *Guatemala: Represión y Resistencia.* (New York, 1980)

Network in Solidarity with the People of Guatemala [NISGUA]. *Guatemala Network News.* Published bi-monthly through 1987; now published bi-monthly as *Report on Guatemala,* jointly with the Guatemala News and Information Bureau [GNIB], (Washington)

Nouwen, Henri J.M. *Love in a Fearful Land: A Guatemalan Story.* Ave Maria Press (Notre Dame, 1985)

Otra Guatemala. A new quarterly review published in Mexico City by Guatemalans. (First issue, August 1987)

Painter, James. *Guatemala: False Hope, False Freedom. The Rich, the Poor and the Christian Democrats.* Catholic Institute for International Relations and Latin America Bureau (Research and Action) Limited (London, 1987)

Peckenham, Nancy. *Guatemala 1983: A Report to the American Friends Service Committee.* (Philadelphia, 1983)

Plenty International. *Guatemala: A Commentary on Human Rights.* (Summertown, 1983)

Polémica. "Informe de la OEA Sobre la Situación de los Derechos Humanos en Guatemala," No. 2 (noviembre-diciembre, 1981). San Jose, Costa Rica)

Secretaria de la Coordinadora de Ayuda a Refugiados Guatemaltecos. *Boletín.* Published at intervals (Mexico City)

Schlesinger, Stephen and Stephen Kinzer. *Bitter Fruit: The Untold Story of the American Coup in Guatemala.* Doubleday (Garden City, 1983)

Women for Guatemala. *Ch'Abuj Ri Ixoc.* [The Voice of the Women]. Published at intervals (Washington) *Guatemala History Told by Its Women.* (Washington, n.d.) *The Truth about Guatemalan Women.* (Washington, n.d.)

Women's International Resource Exchange. *We Continue Forever: Sorrow and Strength of Guatemalan Women.* (New York, 1983)